PRISONS FOR WOMEN
A Practical Guide
to
Administration Problems

PRISONS FOR WOMEN

A Practical Guide
to
Administration Problems

By

JOY S. EYMAN, M.Ed., M.S. Crim.

Formerly, Warden
South Carolina Women's Correctional Institution
Formerly, Warden
Tennessee Prison for Women
Formerly, Detective
Criminal Division
Hillsborough County Sheriff's Department
Tampa, Florida

CHARLES C THOMAS • PUBLISHER
Springfield • Illinois • U.S.A.

Published and Distributed Throughout the World by
CHARLES C THOMAS • PUBLISHER

BANNERSTONE HOUSE
301-327 East Lawrence Avenue, Springfield, Illinois, U.S.A.
NATCHEZ PLANTATION HOUSE
735 North Atlantic Boulevard, Fort Lauderdale, Florida, U.S.A.

© 1971, by CHARLES C THOMAS • PUBLISHER
Library of Congress Catalog Card Number: 71-130924

With THOMAS BOOKS *careful attention is given to all details of
manufacturing and design. It is the Publisher's desire to present books
that are satisfactory as to their physical qualities and artistic possibilities
and appropriate for their particular use.* THOMAS BOOKS *will be true
to those laws of quality that assure a good name and good will.*

Printed in the United States of America
W-2

To my mother

MRS. C. H. SATTERWHITE

PREFACE

I FIRST BECAME interested in the field of corrections when I was appointed warden of a state prison for women. I found the position both a challenge and a frustration. The challenge remains constant, many frustrations remain also. I have been able to eliminate the frustration of being without an education in corrections. However, most persons who work in corrections have not been afforded this opportunity. For this reason I have written this book.

The book is simply a practical guide for those who, like myself, become workers within a prison, yet have no background in the correctional philosophy. I have had personal opportunity to test the value of most of the suggestions recommended.

I am indebted to my family and many of my friends for their help. My dear friends, Mrs. J. G. McRae and Miss Brownie MacAllister, have had unlimited faith in me. If the Tropical Bank and Trust Company had not also had faith in me I would have remained without my education in corrections. Dr. George Killinger has furnished me, through his classes, a good deal of the material used in the chapters on "Classification" and "The Correctional Trilogy." Dr. Roger K. Kalina has written "Management of the Psychopath." My three daughters, Terry Lou, Judy, and Gretchen, have survived my two terms as prison warden and have grown into lovely, law-abiding citizens. My mother has also survived the shock of her daughter going to prison, not once, but twice!

INTRODUCTION

THIS BOOK IS written as a practical guide for the administration of women's prisons. Most of the chapters in this book concern the specific areas in which women's institutions differ from institutions for men. The principles laid down in the *Manual of Correctional Standards,* issued by the American Correctional Association, are adhered to where applicable.

All institutions for women have difficult problems because they must accept offenders ranging in age from teen-age girls to senile women, who present a wide range of sentences and offenses, personality traits, backgrounds, mentalities, and training and treatment needs.

It is both a challenge and a disadvantage that institutions for women must be all things to all people. In most states, it is possible to provide at least two institutions for men, one of the prison and one of the reformatory type, plus various types of minimum-custody honor camps. Because women represent a small proportion of the total inmate population (about thirty men to every one woman), only one state provides more than one state facility for female offenders. Even this is on the basis of geography and population distribution rather than differential functioning.

The first separate institution for women in the United States, the Indiana Women's Prison, was opened in 1873. During the next forty years, only four more were opened: the Massachusetts Prison (Massachusetts Correctional Institution for Women at Framingham) in 1877, the New York Reformatory for Women (Westfield Farm) in 1901, the District of Columbia Women's Reformatory in 1910, and the New Jersey Reformatory for Women in 1913. Fifty-one years later there are only twenty-nine separate institutions for women, including one in Puerto Rico, the District of Columbia Reformatory for Women, and one Federal Institution.

Of the twenty-nine existing facilities for women which are completely separate and have their own warden or superintendent, nineteen institutions have less than 200 inmates, ten have less than 100 and the remaining ten range from 200 to 878.[1] The problems of the small institution must therefore be recognized.

Institutions for women present some differing characteristics which should also be recognized. Even more than male populations, the inmates of women's institutions reflect variations relative to geographical location. For example, the smaller, inland, more rural state is less likely to produce a large number of inmates with narcotic problems, and states which are in the process of change through immigration or emigration present problems different from those of a state remaining fairly stable. In some states, many misdemeanors carry sentences to women's reformatory, while in others, the inmates are mostly felons.

In too many instances, women prisoners are housed in combined institutions which are primarily designed for male inmates. This is poor practice, and it is urged that all possible effort be made to correct this situation where it exists. Where small numbers of female inmates make it economically unsound to establish separate institutions, it is recommended by the Women's Correctional Association that states join together to establish an institution for female offenders from the participating states. The Council of State Governments has indicated a precedent for such a movement and could be helpful in planning regional institutions for women. The practice of housing women inmates in male institutions is so strongly disapproved that standards for such situations have been purposely omitted from the *Manual of Correctional Standards*.

Some women's institutions have made notable contributions to penology. Several of them are rated as among the best institutions for either men or women in the country. Unfortunately, many institutions for women are a shameful disgrace. These states are surely guilty of criminal neglect.

J. S. E.

---

[1] *Directory of State and Federal Institutions*, 1964.

CODE OF ETHICS FOR A PRISON WARDEN

As warden of a prison, I am a servant of those who look to me for help and guidance which will restore the integrity of their personality. My motivation must be toward how I can serve this person; how this action of mine, this decision of mine, this order of mine may contribute to the solution of the problems of the persons placed in my care.

The reformation of the prisoner is the ideal toward which I strive. My goal is to restore that facet of a man's personality, the absense of which detracts from his human dignity.

I am not dealing with a perfect human being, but with one who, in one way or another, has been scarred by life, has wandered away from the social mores. It becomes my high destiny to see whether I can remove the scars and return him, with the perfection he should have, back to society.

As I deal with this man, the negligence of others does not entitle me to endanger the priceless dignity of the human personality by actions performed in ignorance. What knowledge I have not received by formal training, I must try to acquire by private study.

I have been chosen for a tremendous task, and I must be willing to put forth unceasing effort to be worthy of the honor. Not to do so is to be unfaithful to the trust society has placed in me.

J. S. E.

CONTENTS

PRISONS FOR WOMEN

A Practical Guide

to

Administration Problems

Chapter 1

CLASSIFICATION

T HE TERM "CLASSIFICATION" is a confusing one because it is used to denote more than one type of procedure.

One meaning of the term is used to denote a disciplinary status, such as trustee. This type of classification is discussed in more detail in Chapter 9. Another meaning of "classification" is to denote types of prisons. This classification among prisons applies to male prisons and is ranked according to degrees of security. This classification is explained in more detail in Chapter 13. Yet another meaning of the term is the classification of inmates for assignment in study and work programs and in institutional housing. It is this type of classification that will be discussed in detail in this chapter.

ADMISSION AND ORIENTATION PROGRAM

The period immediately following commitment presents a most critical time from the standpoint of institutional adjustment and also a most opportune time for the initiation of treatment—if the inmate has had her immediate worries allayed. Most inmates enter the institution with fears, resentment, misconceptions, and frustrations. They face months or years of confinement and have fear of what may happen to them while confined—fear for their children's welfare, fear of the prospect of broken ties with family and friends, and fear of the problems they will face upon eventual return to the community.

Obviously, persons who are preoccupied with such anxieties are not in a frame of mind to enter upon a program of self-improvement. These problems that need immediate attention must be taken care of on a first priority basis. Already too much time has elpased since the inmate was removed from the home

3

environment. These high-priority items which should have been taken care of immediately after the inmate was incarcerated in the county jail must now be taken care of by the prison staff. This is the first step in winning the confidence of the inmate and in helping her to help herself.

From the moment the inmate enters prison, she is being prepared for her return to society. Few inmates bring with them any reality-based understanding of the correctional program or any real hope of profiting from this experience. Most have erroneous preconceptions gained from other prisoners while in jail awaiting trial and commitment.

The reception period immediately following admission to prison is therefore of great significance. Intimate and skilled counseling is especially necessary to help the inmate start her efforts to gain insight into her situation and to accept what she herself must do about it.

During the initial (orientation) period in the institution, a separate, self-contained unit is desirable—a unit which will provide most of the elements of the total program. There are a number of advantages in keeping the new inmate separated from the main population for a time. Segregation is advisable for medical reasons. Also, a thoroughgoing diagnostic program makes a period of segregation advisable in order that the new inmate will be available for interview and examinations. Here the newly committed woman is oriented to the total philosophy, policies, rules, programs, and spare-time activities of the institution and what is expected of her. Without an orientation program, new inmates receive their orientation from other inmates— this could be from the more criminally and institutionally sophisticated and disgruntled ones. This type of orientation immediately sets up a barrier between the personnel and re-habilitative influences on one side and the inmate population on the other.

For the woman who has never before been in prison, there is much she needs to know, not only about prison regulations, practices, and organizations but also about the treatment and training opportunities available. To the woman who has been confined previously, her past institutional experiences may have established uncooperative attitudes which must be changed before she will accept assistance or enter into a constructive program. This reception period should be seen as one of information and sharing between staff and inmate designated to set the tone for the period of incarceration and to develop mutual acceptance.

The physical setting of the admission procedures should, by its cleanliness, attractiveness, and cheerfulness, reflect the tone of the institution. Staff members involved in the admitting procedures should be selected because of their ability to relate with a newly committed woman in a warm, understanding, professional, and limit-setting manner so that she sees the institution as one which accepts her as an individual whose human dignity should be preserved and protected during the correctional process, while at the same time setting an expectation that she will be responsible for her own adult behavior while in the institution.

The actual examination of commitment papers, preparation of receipts, and handling of other legal matters should be done promptly, quietly, and efficiently so as to be able to turn attention as quickly as possible to the newly committed woman herself.

Fingerprinting, photographing, inventorying of personal property, bathing, examination for contraband, initial physical examination, and issuing of clothing should be handled in a manner as nonthreatening as possible, with efforts made to protect the woman's privacy and dignity.

The essentials of a good orientation program include the following:

1. Separate buildings for housing.
2. Thorough search for contraband.
3. Immediate physical to guard against the spread of contagious diseases.
4. Diagnostic tests for syphillis, diabetes, tuberculosis, cancer (Pap smear), etc.
5. Medical and dental recommendations regarding corrective therapy, etc.
6. Psychological diagnosis through the following tests:
    a. General intelligence.
        (1) Army Alpha, Otis, Bellvue-Wechsler, Binet-Simon, etc.

    b. Projective Personality Tests.
      (1) Rorschach.
      (2) Cornell Index. Minnesota Multiphasic.
      (3) Introvert-Extrovert.
    c. Stanford Achievement (grade placement), or the Gray-Votaw-Rogers (GVR) General Achievement Test.
    d. Vocational Aptitude.
      (1) Stenquist.
      (2) Form Boards, etc.
    e. Interest.
      (1) Strong's, etc.
    f. Masculine-Females Index.
    g. Koh's Ethical.
    h. Allport (attitude).

7. Psychiatric diagnosis through routine interview to determine presence of the following:
    a. Psychosis.
    b. Psychopathic characteristics.
    c. Epilepsy.
    d. Migraine.
    e. Sleepwalking.
    f. Neurotic and hypochondrical tendencies.
    g. Assignment to psychotherapy.

8. Special interview with vocational counselor to determine vocational skills and plan for institutional vocational training.
    a. Skills as related to present offense and community needs and opportunities (don't give a Dale Carnegie Course to a psychopath, nor a Graphoanalysis Course to forgers!).
    b. Analysis of aptitude test and interests as expressed by inmate.

9. Educational interview to determine academic needs.
    a. If tests below 5.0 grade, required to attend academic school.
    b. Related trade classes.
    c. Special cultural classes in journalism, home economics, languages, business administration, social sciences, etc.
    d. Social study groups and town hall meetings.
    e. Publishing of inmate magazine as means of inmate expressions.

10. Social service interview obtaining information for:
    a. Social history.
    b. Admission summary.
    c. Classification report.
    d. Mail regulations.
    e. Early release planning.
    f. Visiting rules and regulations.

11. Outline to inmate of custody, housekeeping, and work programs.

12. Explanation of the plant facilities and opportunities.
13. Function and use of the library explained.
14. Religious activities.
    a. Talks to all inmates in orientation by Catholic, Protestant, and Jewish chaplains.
15. Recreational activities.

ADMISSION SUMMARY

The admission summary results from all the data assembled by the probation officer, the investigation agencies, and the social welfare groups. Each department participates, but the social service department is responsible for assembly of the material. Each admission summary includes the presentence investigation plus the work of all personnel in the orientation period.

All pertinent information should be verified by reliable sources, particularly where information is likely to be damaging to the inmate and her family or may have a definite bearing on the welfare of the community. Verifications preferably should be obtained in documentary forms (letters, photostat copies, certified statements, etc.). In each instance, it should be clearly stated whether important information is verified or unverified.

The admission summary should consist of the following:

1. *The present offense.* Details are given as to time, place, circumstances, and nature of the crime, with particular reference to the exact parts played by the inmate and her associates, if any; date and place of arrest, arresting officers, plea, place of detention, bond, number of days in custody, statement of officers, codefendents, complainants, witnesses, present status of codefendents, inmate's own statement, and inmate's attitude toward offense. The part played by codefendents is important, whether in or out of prison, since criminal associates are an important factor in the life and inclinations of the subject.
2. *Prior record.* Listed in this section is a factual chronological record of the inmate's prior criminal record. Dates, courts, titles of offenses, and dispositions are verified from the official records and an attempt is made to ascertain and report the inmate's attitudes and feelings (in retrospect) for each prior offense, for whatever insight may be gained thereby into her criminal habits and motivations but with as little editorializing as possible.

3. *Family history.* Names, ages, occupations, etc., of parents are listed here, after investigation and verification. Family attitudes and relationships are explored. Particular reference is made to the home atmosphere in which the inmate has been reared. All data concerning family composition, relationships, standing in the community, etc., are carefully checked against the records of other agencies to which the family may have been known. Where indicated, neighborhood inquiries concerning the family and its members are discreetly made. All sources of information, both within and without the home, are noted. Racial and national derivations are noted, and where the circumstances warrant it, the family tree may be examined to obtain data on those factors in the family inheritance that may have had effect upon its social conditioning or that of the inmate.

Brothers and sisters also come in for attention, with as much biographical and identifying detail on each as seems desirable. This information is of special value in regulating visiting privileges and as a factor in promoting prison morale. It is also a vital resource as a check against the possibility of escape. Attitudes and relationships of the various relatives toward the inmate are gone into, as well as her toward them. Any past or present psychopathologic or criminal taints are noted for whatever bearing they may have on the family interrelationships or in understanding the inmate's situation in regard to them.

Where no immediate family relatives are available for interview, special efforts should be made through cooperating agencies elsewhere to run them down and secure the desired verifications and other items of information. If this effort is unsuccessful or if no near relatives exist, attempts should be made to get in touch with next of kin. If the inmate requests that no contact at all be made with relatives, her motives should be carefully explored and probably should be judiciously overridden.

If the inmate is married or has been, the names, ages, and other identifying data on spouses and ex-spouses are recorded, as are those of children resulting from the unions. Appropriate verifications are made of marriages, separations, and divorces. Spouses and ex-spouses should always be interviewed, but approaches to children, especially minor children, are always delicately undertaken.

4. *Home and neighborhood.* This section is devoted to a description of the home surroundings of the inmate at the time of arrest and the period immediately preceding it. The physical arrangements, rent, furnishings, etc., are described, with particular attention to atmosphere. If the inmate owns the home, its value

and her equity in it are recorded. Neighborhood influences, others in the household and their relationships to the family are all explored, as well as information concerning previous addresses.

5. *Education.* This includes the age at which the inmate entered school; grade completed, type of school, school adjustment, age and the reason for withdrawal from school, and attitude toward school. If the inmate was employed in this period, the necessary verifications are made with appropriate data on earnings, skills, job adjustments and tenures, earning capacity, savings, etc.

6. *Religion.* Reference is made to the inmate's interest in, and attitude toward, religious observance. If she has been baptized or confirmed, the appropriate certificates are examined and the details noted. If the inmate is unaffiliated with or has defected from any organized religious group, an effort is made to ascertain what ethical or other standards serve her in lieu of a religious belief.

7. *Interests and activities.* Leisure-time pursuits, hobbies, organization affiliations, associates, special abilities, ambitions, and achievements are covered in this section.

8. *Mental and physical health.* The general health of the inmate throughout her life is discussed in this section, with special reference to any serious illnesses or hospitalization she may have undergone. Results of recent physical and mental examinations, intelligence tests, etc., are assembled in verified form. Special attention is paid to remedial physical defects and also to any organic or other ailments that may have in any way influenced the inmate's behavior.

9. *Employment.* This includes a review of employment covering approximately the past ten years, employer, kind of work, earnings, duration, reasons for leaving, adjustment, attitude of employer, social security number, and history of welfare relief.

10. *Resources.* This includes property, insurance, investments, compensations, pensions, rentals, savings, income from other sources, and financial obligations.

11. *Agencies interested.* It is quite helpful to list those agencies known to, and interested in, the inmate. It may be desirable to list the social service exchange or county welfare board registrations and clearances. The following is a suggested format:

Social Service Exchange Registrations

Family Welfare	8 - 1956	(cleared)
Salvation Army	10 - 1954	(cleared)
Municipal Hospital	6 - 1953	
Juvenile Court	7 - 1960	(cleared)

Others Interviewed
St. Paul's Church (received letter)
Y.W.C.A. (interviewed)
Polk Junior College (transcript of record)

12. *Summary.* This is an evaluative summary and analysis of the factual information heretofore reported. This includes an analysis of contributing factors which led to the present offense, a summary and interpretation of inmate's problems and needs, and an evaluation of inmate's personality. Sources of information to be used in developing the admission summary are suggested at the end of this chapter.

13. *Recommendations or plan.* The admission summary becomes a practical document when the final page is devoted to a listing of recommendations in the above area of diagnostic study for the inmate's institutional and parole program.

The orientation period, lasting from two to four weeks, ends with the classification conference.

CLASSIFICATION CONFERENCE

The conference of the classification committee provides the inmate with an opportunity to build up a sense of confidence through participation in formulating her own program. An informal atmosphere during the conference will obtain best results.

The classification committee usually consists of the superintendent, the assistant superintendent, the director of education, the guidance supervisor, the parole supervisor, and the ranking custodial officer.

After orientation, inmates are assigned quarters and become members of the institution community. They are entitled to its privileges: church, school, employment, movies, and other group activities. These privileges may be forfeited, however, by antisocial behavior—which is also the rule of life outside the institution.

RECLASSIFICATION

Reclassification may occur at any time. Occasionally at the initial classification, a tentative date may be set for reclassification. However, if no date is set, reclassification may occur for the following reasons:

1. Institutional needs.
2. Vocational or educational training.
3. Family assistance through assignment to paying industries.
4. Miscellaneous reasons such as escape risk, medical care, etc.

PRERELEASE PLANNING

Prerelease programming is a part of the institution's overall correctional effort. It cannot be isolated from other treatment activities. Preparation for release should begin at the time of sentencing or even before, with the preparation of the pre-sentence investigation. This preparation for release is primarily an institutional problem. Successful preparation depends upon an individualized training and treatment program based upon a complete diagnostic study of each inmate.

Every opportunity must be afforded the inmate to improve herself physically, mentally, vocationally, and spiritually while she is incarcerated. The prison must help the inmate to develop self-understanding, to realize what in her makeup caused her to use poor judgment in the past. Every opportunity must be made to help the inmate help herself. Every person on the staff, from the custodial officer to the psychiatrist, must be an effective therapist. For effective therapy, the staff member must have a sincere interest in the inmate and a hopeful attitude toward inmate problems.

The parole-supervising agency has a right to expect the following from parole boards:

1. Women who have benefitted from training available in the institution.
2. Women who have grown in their abilities to govern their emotions and impulses.
3. Women able to become a part of the community.

It is known that the greatest number of postprison failures occur within the first two months of an inmate's release. The crucial period of time is the first three weeks. Therefore, something should be done to help inmates bridge the gap between the prison community and life in a free society.

A prerelease program should provide for a period of evaluation in which the experiences of the inmate and the specialized knowledge of the staff may be examined in a final effort to point the way to realistic solutions of the myriad problems facing the woman about to be released. Additionally, opportunity should be given the prerelease inmate to verbalize her feelings and thoughts about her problems.

The prerelease program used at the United States Penitentiary,[1] Lewisburg, Pennsylvania, might give some ideas for establishing such a program at a women's prison. However, because of the small size of most women's prisons, the group activities mentioned in the Lewisburg project would, of necessity, be adapted to individual usage. While a group approach is beneficial in several ways—not the least being conservation of staff time—it must always be regarded only as supplemental to individual planning with each prerelease inmate.

The following three principles were recognized at Lewisburg as being essential in establishing a realistic program of prerelease preparation:

1. To make available to prerelease inmates information and assistance deemed pertinent in release planning.
2. To provide each prerelease inmate the opportunity, in a nonthreatening situation, to discuss problems and anxieties relating to her release and future social adjustment.
3. To provide a system of evaluating the effectiveness of release planning procedures.

A part of the program's approach was taken from the basic premises of the Alcoholics Anonymous. To the prerelease inmate is presented this proposition: You accept that release to the community will pose problems of varying kind and degree, you have a sincere desire to avoid further delinquency, you are resolved that you do not wish to undergo again the experience of confinement, you wish to begin the basis of a sound future. Having acknowledged these things, you want help from others. Prerelease planning can be a part of the answer to your needs. The remainder of the answer lies within you in your own

---

[1] Baker, J. E.: "Preparing prisoners for their return to the community." *Federal Probation*, June, 1966, pp. 43-50.

capacities and your sincere willingness to utilize them for your self-betterment.

Throughout the program emphasis is placed on the individual's responsibility for her future. The role of the staff can be, at best, no more than supportive and the measure of success no greater than the individual's most sincere efforts.

This prerelease program provides intensive preparation in three categories: mandatory considerations, planning and resources, and emotional factors, each comprised as follows:

1. Mandatory consideration
   a. Legal aspects
      (1) Statutory provisions concerning mandatory release and parole
      (2) Civil rights and responsibilities
      (3) Release to other custody
   b. Administrative aspects
      (1) Rules of supervision
      (2) Role of the parole officer
      (3) Destination determination
      (4) Clearance procedures
2. Planning and resources
   a. Employment information and counseling
      (1) Job responsibilities
      (2) State Bureau of Employment services
   b. Financial planning
      (1) Gratuity allowance
      (2) Disposition of personal funds
      (3) Discharge clothing
      (4) Transportation
   c. Community resources
      (1) Clergy
      (2) Community agencies (Travelers Aid, Family Service, Salvation Army, etc.)
      (3) Alcoholic's Anonymous
3. Emotional factors
   a. Common social problems
      (1) Race relations
      (2) Highway safety
      (3) Credit-installment buying
   b. Attitudinal problems
      (1) A series of discussion groups providing opportunity for a review of possible readjustment problems

To provide the staff with leads as to the major concerns of the prerelease inmate, a questionnaire can be designed to obtain insight into the prerelease inmate's attitude toward chances for successful social adjustment, immediate postrelease problems, anticipated readjustment problems, and analysis of prison experience.

A summary analysis of responses from Lewisburg revealed the average prerelease inmate to be principally interested in finding a job and having money to meet release needs. He also had a strong wish for assistance from the institution. As the inmate viewed the situation ninety days prior to his release, his principal and immediate postrelease interest was to "settle down and stay out of trouble." His anticipated major problem was finding adequate employment and/or financial assistance. He had no real fear of nonacceptance by his family, but did express some uncertainty. He anticipated some difficulty with former friends but nothing of consequence. From society at large, he expressed the hope for acceptance. He had no antagonism toward the institution, expressing the feeling that the confinement experience was an expensive lesson, usually deserved.

On the basis of the Lewisburg study, some of the factors which may be of value in formulation of a prerelease program are presented here.

In 78 percent of the cases in which there was definite employment at release, severance had occurred usually within ninety days.[2] Further, 85 percent of respondents were employed six months following release. While the value of a job in hand at time of release cannot be debated, it might be a more judicious use of staff effort to focus on equipping the individual to hold a job.

Where a prerelease inmate verbalized an apprehension regarding getting postrelease employment, there was usually conjured the spectre of employer prejudice and adverse public opinion. Experience and reason showed that neither of these was a major obstacle to obtaining a job. Such an apprehension can be interpreted in most instances as an admission of a social lack—the inability, due to insufficient knowledge, to not only

---

[2] *Ibid.*, p. 49.

get a job, but more importantly, a fear of not knowing how to hold it. This has significance for institutional training efforts, as it indicates a need for increased emphasis on job-relationships with peers and supervisors, as well as on job-finding methods.

This brings us face to face with a characteristic common to prison inmates—a low frustration tolerance with the corollary of limited perseverance in the face of almost any obstacle. The foregoing is further borne out by some interesting facts found at Lewisburg. Wherever a released inmate was referred to a state employment service, a union, or a prospective employer, a letter of introduction was always given him. Fifty percent made the initial contact, but when a job was not immediately available, few reported back for further interview.[3]

SOURCES OF INFORMATION

Duplication of work in procuring background information on inmates should be avoided wherever possible. Therefore, several suggestions are presented as resources available to the prison personnel upon request. These include both informal sources of information and information from correctional-oriented agencies.

Informal Information Resources

Many times the first knowledge the staff has that a woman has been committed to the prison is when she is being escorted to the door of the prison. Sometimes a case will have enough notoriety to be in the newspapers, thereby giving advance notice that the woman is supposed to reach the prison at some un-designated time.

The new inmate is often escorted to the prison with only the court commital papers. These state only the crime for which she was found guilty and the length of her sentence.

What of her social history? her children? her disposition? So many things need to be known about this person who has been sent to the prison, and many of these things need to be known immediately.

------

[3] *Ibid.*, p. 49.

Information From Transporting Officer

The transportation officer can often furnish valuable information about the inmate, her family, and her crime. Many times the transportation officer is a deputy sheriff who has worked actively on this case. He knows the inmate and her family situation well and any mitigating circumstances of the crime that may not be brought out in official records.

Most of the law enforcement officers that I have known have had great compassion for inmates. Rarely have I found a vindictive officer, and if so, it is well to examine his reasons. The inmate who does not arouse some degree of compassion in a law enforcement officer is an inmate that will probably give a great deal of trouble.

A perfect opening for good public relations can be developed with the transportation officer. So often, police, probation, and prison officials, who are all working for the same goal with the same person, do not have any contact with each other. This is a handicap for all concerned.

When the transportation officer arrives at the prison with a new inmate, invite him to have coffee or dinner with some designated officer so that he might be shown the prison and have the program explained to him. Few transporting officers are familiar with the prison and its program. If he becomes familiar with these operations, he will be able to allay some of the fears of those other inmates he will be transporting.

Let the officer know that you value his opinion of the new inmate he has just transported and that you wish to learn as much as possible about her and her family.

There is also the possibility that the officer knows other inmates that you have in custody and can give you valuable information about them.

Since officers in a rural area often know and see the families of inmates, it would be well to let the transportation officer talk to any inmate he knows to give them firsthand news of their families and to take back messages from the inmate. This could be the closest or only link many inmates have with their families and friends.

Social Service Agencies

Most inmates and their families are known to their local welfare board. Here again, the welfare staff can be of great help and are usually most cooperative. They are often able to furnish complete casework reports on the inmate. Furthermore, at the time of the inmate's return to her community, it is the welfare agency that may furnish her guidance and counseling, as well as financial assistance. This department may direct her to an agency that will help her secure a job if she has returned from prison without employment. The welfare agency is as anxious to help keep the inmate employed and self-supporting as you are to see her make good on her return to free life!

When an inmate is released from prison, sometimes outmoded state laws require that she be given a ticket to return her to the place from which she was sentenced, regardless of whether it is her home or not. Traveler's Aid can help these inmates to return to their own families. They may also be able to give the inmate temporary lodging and food while she is locating employment.

Information From Correctional-Oriented Agencies

Presentence Report

This report is prepared by a probation officer before the defendant is sentenced. It is not submitted to the court unless the defendant has pleaded guilty or has been found guilty.

As a rule, the court will consider the presentence report as a confidential document for the court's use alone. However, arrangements may be made with the court that copies be sent to the prison classification officer or social services supervisor.

In order to assume the confidential character of the report, which should be paramount at all times, the probation officer may use a reference code throughout the body of the report and on a separate sheet give the sources according to the code. The same procedure may be followed with reference to confidential information. In following this practice, the confidential information, and the sources as well, are available to the court.

When the report is sent to the institution, the reference code on the separate sheet may be sent under separate cover in an envelope marked "confidential." Each page of the presentence report may be stamped "confidential" in bold letters.

The length of the presentence report will depend largely on the requirements of the court, the nature of the offense, the extent to which complicated factors are present in the defendant's personality makeup, the size of the probation officer's investigation and supervision load, as well as such other factors as geographical considerations, time available to make the investigation, etc.

All pertinent information should be verified by reliable sources, particularly when information is likely to be damaging to the defendant and her family or may have a definite bearing on the welfare of the community. Verifications preferably should be obtained in documentary form (letters, photostat copies, certified statements, etc.). Probation officers should clearly indicate in each instance whether important information is verified or unverified.

The presentence investigation report embraces the following elements, which are, of course, subject to variations of emphasis, depending on the needs and facilities of the courts in the various jurisdictions but which may be regarded as minimum standard practice generally throughout the nation:

1. *Present offense.* Under this heading, the offense (the one actually before the court) is described in narrative fashion. Details are given as to time, place, circumstances, and nature of the crime, with particular reference to the exact parts played by the defendant and her associates, if any. The sequence of events leading up to the arrest is portrayed, as is the manner of the arrest itself. Care is taken to give the source of each item of information, together with the names, addresses, and occupations the complainant, witnesses, and other affected persons, and the name and command of the arresting officer. Repetition of detail is avoided, but if there is more than one version of the circumstances of the crime, the discrepancies are noted and explored. If these cannot be reconciled, they are reported as found, so that the court may determine for itself whether they are important enough to warrant clarification by testimony taking.

2. *Status of codefendants and accomplices.* The part played by

codefendants is noted in this section, together with the disposition or present status of any charges filed against them. As much information as possible is sought and reported concerning unapprehended accomplices, whether their actual identity is known or not. All of this is important in later treatment, whether in or out of prison, since criminal associates are an important factor in the life and inclinations of the subject.

3. *Statement of the defendant.* This section gives the defendant's version of her involvement in the offense. Sometimes, when convicted by verdict, defendants will make no statement at all or will vigorously deny everything and protest their innocence. The investigator accepts whatever statements they care to make, however inconsistent these may be with the facts as he otherwise knows them. This is done to preserve the defendant's rights in the event of appeal. The same procedure is followed with a special classification of young offenders coming within the purview of the Youthful Offender Act (or like statutes) who are investigated, with their written consent and that of their attorneys *before trial* to determine whether a social purpose would be served by not taking them to trial at all. Such youths, in consenting to investigation, do not relinquish their constitutional right to presumption of innocence. Many of them do, however, talk freely if really guilty, since understanding of the beneficial purpose of the investigation (to obviate the stigma or the civil disabilities that often arise in later life from conviction of a criminal offense) is widespread. In "plea of guilty" cases, as described earlier, most defendants readily acknowledge guilt and have little hesitancy in unburdening themselves. Occasionally, however, they hedge their admissions around with all manner of evasion and rationalization. In that case, it is the probation officer's job to use his interviewing skills to cut through the make-believe and the wishful thinking and get at the facts. It is a firmly held theory of correctional work that good confession is, all by itself, an important part of rehabilitation. Consequently, the probation officer makes a special effort to get defendants to "come clean" all the way.

There are, of course, certain categories of offenders, frequently needing psychiatric assistance, who are constitutionally incapable of facing up to or acknowledging responsibility for their acts. They present a keen challenge to the professional diagnostic competency of the probation officer and have a value all their own in that connection.

While ordinarily this phase of the investigation does not have any probative force in settling any lingering questions of innocence or guilt, sometimes it is the decisive factor in resolving just such questions. In rare instances, probation officers have exculpated offenders adjudged guilty in error through flaws in the evidence or improper understanding of the court proceedings. In every case, the judge is kept informed of any snags that occur so that remedial action of one sort or another, if indicated, may be promptly taken.

4. *Attitude of complainant.* Under our American system, criminal offenses are not merely personal crimes; by statutory definition, they are crimes against the whole community. Nevertheless, the complaint of record, the immediate victim of the offense, is a most important figure in the whole proceedings. His feelings with respect to disposition are reported. Sometimes, they have to be thoroughly talked through with him and sometimes fears and obsessions have to be allayed. Not infrequently, the complainant himself is a subject for rehabilitation, financially or for other reasons. Probation officers now consider this effort to be part of their function.

5. *Aggravating and mitigating circumstances.* Pertinent comment is made under this heading to such aspects or consequences of the criminal act as the following:

   a. *For all offenses.* Premeditation or deliberation or the absence of such, whether the offender was a leader or follower or lone operator in the commission of the crime, intoxication or sobriety, resistance to arrest, cooperation with authorities in identification of confederates or in recovering proceeds of crime, apparent repentance or defiance (how sincere?), whether offense was an isolated episode or one of a series, and whether there was provocation, real or imagined, or whether involvement was fortuitous.

   b. *For crimes against the person.* Use of weapons, extent of victim's injuries, permanent or temporary disfigurement, hospitalization, loss of income, etc., aggressiveness of defendant (and perhaps also of complainant).

   c. *For property crimes.* Amount of victim's financial loss or property damage, losses recovered and unrecovered, whether there was insurance coverage; economic circumstances of the complainant (sometimes as contrasted with those of the defendant), extent to which restitution has been or can be made, whether there was a violation of trust or perhaps professional ethics on the part of the defendant.

   d. *For sex crimes.* Age, education, mental condition, reputation, and chastity of victim, whether a social disease was transmitted or a pregnancy ensued, disparity in ages of complainant and defendant.

The foregoing is only an outline. The factors to be described under the heading of "Aggravating and Mitigating Circumstances" are subject to a wide range of variations, depending upon a wide variety of situations; however, this entire section of the presentence investigation report should be written as concisely as possible.

6. *Prior criminal history.* Listed in this section is a factual chronological record of the defendant's prior criminal history. Dates, courts, titles of offenses, and dispositions are verified from the official records and reported together with a brief description of each offense. An effort is made to ascertain and report the defendant's attitudes and feelings (in retrospect) for each prior offense, for whatever insight may be gained thereby into her criminal habits and motivations, but with as little editorializing as possible.

7. *Antecedents and family background.* Names, ages, occupations, etc., of parents are listed here, after investigation and vertification. Family attitudes and relationships are explored (in the appropiate interviews). Particular reference is made to the home atmosphere (felicity, security, health, etc.) in which the defendant has been reared. All data concerning family composition, relationships, standing in the community, etc., are carefully checked against the records of other agencies to which the family may have been known. Probation officers have ready, almost automatic, access to the records of these agencies and are under binding professional agreement to preserve the confidentiality of any information culled from them. Where indicated, neighborhood inquiries concerning the family and its members are discreetly made. All sources of information, both within and without the home, are noted in the text or marginally. Racial and national derivations are noted, and where the circumstances warrant it, the probation officer may go back into the family tree to obtain data on those factors in the family inheritance that may have had any effect upon his social conditioning or that of the defendant.

Brothers and sisters also come in for attention, with as much biographical and identifying detail on each as seems desirable. This information is of special value to prison administrators in regulating visiting privileges and as a factor in promoting prison morale. It is also a vital resource in probation supervision, particularly in cases where the subject has difficult sledding for any reason, and as a check against the possibility of later successful absconding, it is invaluable. Attitudes and relationships of the various relatives toward the defendant are gone into, as well as her's toward them. Any past or present psychopathological or criminal taints are noted for whatever bearing they may have

on the family interrelationships or in understanding the defendant's situation with regard to them.

Where no immediate family relatives are available for interview, special efforts are made through cooperating agencies
elsewhere to run them down and secure the desired verifications
and other items of information. If this effort is unsuccessful or
if no near relatives exist, the officer attempts to get in touch with
next of kin. If the defendant requests that no contact at all be
made with relatives, her motives are carefully explored. In some
cases, it may be expedient or even profitable to respect her
wishes; the more common experience, however, is that they are
best judiciously overridden.

If the defendant is married, or has been, the names, ages,
and other identifying data on spouses and ex-spouses are
recorded, as are those of children resulting from the unions.
Appropriate verifications are made of marriages, separations, and
divorces. Defendant's record as a mother is examined, as are
the causes of any incompatability. Spouses and ex-spouses are
always interviewed, but approaches to children, especially minor
children, are always delicately undertaken.

8. *Developmental history of the defendant*
   a. *Early development history.* All ascertainable data with refer-
      ence to gestation and to pathology at birth or in infancy are
      recorded in this section, together with clinically significant
      incidents of this period.
   b. *School period.* A verified record of conduct and performance
      at elementary school is secured from all the schools the
      defendant attended. The highlights of other phases of the
      defendant's life at this period are also woven into the
      narrative.
   c. *Adolescent period.* High school or college history, if any, is
      obtained and recorded. Stresses and strains of adolescent
      adjustments are explored and reported. If the defendant was
      employed in this period, the necessary verifications are
      made with appropriate data on earnings, skills, job adjust-
      ments and tenures, earning capacity, savings, etc. Informa-
      tion on continuing educational needs and vocational aptitudes
      and goals begins to become important at this stage, as do
      avocational interests and associations outside the home.
   d. *Adult history.* The same type of information as for the
      adolescent period is carried forward into this stage. Military
      service is verified, as is membership in trade unions, fraternal
      organizations, etc.
      The War Department has agreed to verify the military

and medical records of defendants through the Demobilized Personnel Records Branch, Building 105, Records Administration Center, St. Louis, Missouri. The following procedures are suggested in requesting information:

No request should be made until an effort has been made to obtain the desired information from documents in possession of the former soldier, her relatives, family, or the county court records where a photostatic copy of her discharge may have been recorded.

If the probation officer is requesting medical information, records pertaining to treatment received *during military service only* should be requested from the Demobilized Personnel Records Branch, and records pertaining to treatment received *subsequent to military service* should be requested from the Veterans Administration. Moreover, if the officer is aware that the Veterans Administration has requested medical information from the Demobilized Personnel Records Branch for use in a claim initiated by the former soldier, the request for her medical records should be directed to the Veterans Administration, since the records in such cases are retained by that agency.

Throughout the recital of the details of the defendant's life as portrayed in this section and elsewhere in the report, the significance of the various developments to the defendant herself is kept in focus since the really relevant elements in any diagnostic study are not the objective impressions of the investigator but the offender's attitudes and reactions to events and individuals.

9. *Residence arrangements.* This section is devoted to a description of the home surroundings of the defendant at the time of arrest and the period immediately preceding it. The physical arrangement, rent, furnishing, etc., are described, with particular attention to atmosphere. If the defendant owns the home, its value and her equity in it are recorded.

10. *Religion.* Reference is made to the defendant's interest in and attitude toward religious observance. If she has been baptized, confirmed, etc., the appropriate certificates are examined and the details noted. Where the findings disclose a need for stimulation, the pastor is visited or the cooperation of the family is sought. If the defendant is unaffiliated with or has defected from any organized religious group, an exhaustive effort is made to ascertain what ethical or other standards serve her in lieu of a religious belief.

11. *Interests and activities.* Leisure-time pursuits, hobbies, organiza-

tion affiliations, associates, special abilities, ambitions and achievements are all included here.

12. *Mental and physical health.* The general health of the defendant throughout her life is discussed in this section, with special reference to any serious illnesses or hospitalization she may have undergone. Results of recent physical or mental examinations, intelligence tests, etc., are assembled in verified form. In courts having their own clinical psychiatric facilities, almost all defendants undergo some form of psychiatric diagnostic testing; the other courts do the best they can in this direction. In all courts, whether served by house clinics or not, it is fairly standard practice to refer all defendants whose criminal conduct has been abnormal *in se* for extended psychiatric observation, on an inpatient basis, which sometimes lasts for weeks. The statutes make such referrals mandatory for certain categories of offenders as a prerequisite to sentence.

Separate reports are usually furnished to the courts by the examining psychiatrists on all such referrals. It is always well to introduce such reports, in condensed form if necessary, into the probation report proper. Other psychiatric referrals are made where necessary or desirable and where the facilities permit, on a voluntary basis if possible and by formal order of the court if necessary. With or without such referrals, the records of other agencies are always scrutinized for medical and psychiatric data on the defendant and members of her family. Special attention is paid throughout the presentence investigation to remediable physical defects and also to any organic or other ailments that may have in any way influenced the defendant's behavior.

13. *Employment.* This is a review of employment covering approximately the past ten years: employer, kind of work, earnings, duration, reasons for leaving, adjustment, and attitude of employer. This also includes social security number and history of welfare relief.

14. *Resources.* Property, insurance, investments, compensations, pensions, rentals, savings, income from other sources. Financial obligations.

15. *Evaluative summary and analysis of the factual information heretofore reported.* As a general rule, the diagnostic (as distinguished from the fact-gathering) interview with the defendant is deferred until the investigator can face his subject with an already verified accumulation of data on her whole background. It is much easier, under such circumstances, to appraise her statements, to ward off any attempts to take the

interview into unproductive or erraic channels, and in general to get down to "brass tacks." At this point, the defendant is confronted with both the favorable and unfavorable information that has been uncovered concerning her and is given the opportunity to accept, explain, evade, or reject whatever is discussed. It is at this point also that she is briefed on the purposes of the investigation and prepared for as philosophical an acceptance as possible of her current and projected situation.

There is no ready format into which a description of this section of the presentence report may be compressed. The content may be, and usually is, as varied as the idiosyncrasies of the given defendant or the ramifications of her activities. Much depends also on the diagnostic and reporting skills of the investigator. The idea is to evoke insights and perceptions into the defendant's motivations and potentials, as far as possible out of her own reactions to the matters presented to her.

As a professional person, the investigator is also expected to analyze the objective data presented to him during the entire investigation. When possible, the sources and authorities should be given for all conclusions reached. The rules permit impressions to be given out of the investigator's training or experience, or out of his intuitive reasoning, but they must always be clearly labeled as such.

16. *Plan.* This section of the outline has reference to the tentative plan of treatment which the probation officer proposes. It is up to the probation officer to determine whether he wants to set forth his plan in the presentence report or on a separate page. In some instances where the plan contains privileged information, probation officers are inclined to keep the "plan" apart from the regular report. If the presentence report contains confidential information and is mailed to an institution in the case of commitment, it should be clearly indicated on some prominent part of the report that the information is "confidential."

SUMMARY

Classification as discussed in this chapter pertains to the classification of inmates for assignment in study and work programs.

The initial or orientation period immediately following admission to prison is of great significance. During the orientation period, a complete case study is made on the inmate while she is being introduced to the institution's program and regulations.

A classification conference is held with the inmate to help her select the best program suited to her needs. After orientation, inmates are assigned quarters and become members of the institution community. They are entitled to its privileges: church, school, employment, movies, and other group activities. These privileges may be forfeited, however, by antisocial behavior—which is also the rule of life outside the institution.

Reclassification may occur at any time and for various reasons.

Prerelease programming is a part of the institution's overall correctional effort. Successful preparation depends upon an individualized training and treatment program based upon a complete diagnostic study of each inmate. Since the crucial period of time for the inmate is the first three weeks after release, something should be done to help inmates bridge the gap between the prison community and life in a free society.

The following three principles seem to be essential in establishing a realistic program of prerelease preparation:

1. To make available to prerelease inmates information and assistance deemed pertinent in release planning.
2. To provide each prerelease inmate the opportunity, in a non-threatening situation, to discuss problems and anxieties relating to her release and future social adjustment.
3. To provide a system of evaluating the effectiveness of release planning procedures.

The prerelease program should provide intensive preparation in three categories:

1. Mandatory considerations.
2. Planning and resources.
3. Emotional factors.

A study at the United States Penitentiary at Lewisburg, Pennsylvania, revealed that in 78 percent of the cases in which there was definite employment at release, severance had occurred usually within ninety days and further, that 85 percent of respondents were employed six months following release. While the value of a job in hand at time of release cannot be debated, it might be a more judicious use of staff effort to focus on equipping the individual to hold a job.

Duplication of work in procuring background information on inmates should be avoided whenever possible. Therefore, several suggestions are presented as resources available to the prison personnel upon request. One of the most available, and often most valuable, sources of information about the inmate may be the officer who transports the prisoner to the prison. Often the transportation officer has actively investigated the inmate's case and knows her and her family situation quite well and can furnish information that is sorely needed.

BIBLIOGRAPHY

Baker, J. E.: Preparing prisoners for their return to the community. *Federal Probation*, June, 1966, pp. 43-50.

Chapter 2

PERSONNEL

QUALITY OF STAFF is the most important factor in a women's institution.[1] The success of the institution depends primarily upon the personnel. This is a greater challenge in institutions for women because of the involvement in the total program which is required of all staff members. Each individual contributes a vital part to the climate of the institution.

However, one almost universal need of all prisons is more and better staffing. There are still too many jurisdictions where the thought seems to be that anyone can be a custodial officer. The folly of that notion is evident when one recalls that the modern institutional program is a complex one in which all of the latest knowledge of the nature of mankind and the newest techniques must be employed, where the superintendent or warden is looked to for inspiration and guidance, and where each custodial officer is not simply a guard but a member of the team.

The people involved in the selection and appointment process must therefore take particular care to screen out not only the incompetent and untrustworthy but also the overindulgent and gullible, the suspicious and punitive, the neurotic and unstable. Because of the close contact between inmates and staff, it is necessary to identify and remove any staff member who is detrimental to the goals of the program.

PERSONAL INFLUENCE OF STAFF MEMBERS

Never underestimate the power of the staff! Glaser has made a study[2] which reveals the magnitude of the effect the

---

[1] American Correctional Association, *Manual of Correctional Standards.* New York, American Correctional Association, 1966, p. 563.

[2] Glaser, Daniel: *The Effectiveness of a Prison and Parole System.* New York, Bobbs-Merrill, 1964.

entire staff has upon inmates. Although this study was conducted exclusively in male prisons, using male inmates and personnel, it is as applicable to female institutions. The findings and conclusions of this study should be carefully considered for use within women's prisons.

A variety of social and psychological research confirms the proposition that people most often acquire someone else's attitudes if they like him and less often acquire them if they dislike him. If the staff is to compete successfully with the criminal associates of an inmate and inspire anticriminal values, being liked certainly is a major staff asset, although not a guarantee of success.

A necessary condition, if not alone sufficient, for a staff member's favorable influence upon an inmate appears to be the capacity to treat the inmate pleasantly. Such an attitude conveys to the inmate the notion that she is accepted as a person even when her attitudes or actions are opposed. There is ample evidence that control can be achieved by staff without a hostile or superior attitude, and that positive leadership and influence is difficult to achieve without at least a minimum of friendliness and respect.

The most frequently cited[3] type of reason for disliking an officer was his manner of expressing himself toward inmates, rather than specific things he did. This is one of many kinds of evidence suggesting the importance to the offenders of their self-esteem and the difficulty of influencing them in a desired fashion if one fails to take into account their need to defend whatever favorable conception they may have of themselves or to achieve a still more favorable self-conception.

Staff influence on inmates varies directly with the staff's showing the inmate the same type of personal behavior that causes a man to be liked or disliked in nonprison relationships. Inmates are most influenced by staff who act towards them in a friendly and considerate, rather than hostile, tone and manner. Inmates are also most influenced by staff who treat them with fairness and predictability.

---

[3] *Ibid.*, p. 132.

It was found that the officers who the men credited as having been rehabilitative influences gave the inmates self-respect. This did not mean that the officers were unusually lenient, lax, or permissive; it meant only that they treated the men with a personal interest and without pretension or condescension. The officers were friendly in a way that inspired confidence and respect rather than contempt; they were frank, fair, and considerate.

It is impressive in the Glaser study how often the inmate's regard and respect for the officer was cemented by the officer's maintaining the same attitude and availability to the inmate outside of prison as in. The small voluntary gestures of some officers—taking a man to the train or bus or corresponding with him—seemed to confirm that the officer was not false in his gestures of interest and respect in the prison.

In some state prisons, there is often an especially rigid prohibition of employee familiarity with released prisoners, which stems from certain custodial bogeymen. Officials enforcing such a restriction harp on a few isolated incidents in past decades in which some untrained staff, appointed through political patronage, were induced by released prisoners or inmate relatives to smuggle things in or out of the prison. These fears continue to influence policy.

Prison security seems aided not so much by nonfraternization rules as by the staff's inculcation with the goals of the prison service, with normal responsibility, and with sufficient sophistication regarding criminal machinations to prevent their being "conned" too readily.

California prisons have even found it worthwhile to have their employees bring successful ex-inmates back to prison to counsel inmates nearing release, and this also has been done in some federal prisons. Moreover, the custodial security record in federal prisons probably is better than that of the states with rigid nonfraternization rules.

Custodial officers can be said to have the greatest total impact everywhere if the impact is measured as the sum of most liked and most disliked. This suggests the significance of their job in terms of potential for favorable or unfavorable influence.

Custodial and work-supervision personnel were the staff whom inmates most often credited with helping them. It is striking that about 90 percent do not mention vocational teaching by the work supervisors; instead, they stress only their personal relationships to the work supervisor.

The work supervisor not only is responsible for maintaining custody and order, but he also is concerned with training, with making individual work reports, and with innumerable other duties involving him in daily personal relationships with a relatively small number of inmates.

The "treatment personnel" had the distinction of being least frequently the most disliked, but their relatively low frequency of selection for either the liked or disliked designation suggests that they have less influence than other staff on the prison experience of most inmates. Of course, if they nevertheless change the abilities of inmates markedly, they could still most affect the inmate's postrelease experience. The parole officers or case-workers were more often designated the most disliked than the most liked staff members, but like the teachers, chaplains, and clinical staff, their overall selection as either most liked or disliked was not great.

The treatment staff are predominately disliked on the basis of their negative response to requests. They differ from the other disliked categories of staff in much less frequently being accused of hostile mannerisms.

It is interesting to find that inmate contact with institutional social workers is very much a function of the inmate's educational attainment. It seems that the higher educational level of institution caseworkers, compared with most of the remainder of the prison staff, may impair the caseworker's ability to communicate with inmates who are of low education. Also, inmates with less education may be more ill at ease in the formal interview situation where casework contacts occur and may therefore less frequently initiate such contact.

The distinctive feature of responses on the treatment staff from inmates of five federal prisons was the infrequency with which treatment staff were mentioned as either the most liked or the most disliked. This suggests that these personnel have less total impact on inmates than might be expected from the emphasis on treatment as the main function of these modern prisons.

The evidence collected by Glaser suggests that prison staff could easily achieve a much greater influence on a larger proportion of inmates than they now affect if the prison employees focused their attention on the following two principles:

1. The prison employee who has the greatest reformative influence on an offender is the one who is able to demonstrate sincere and sustained concern for, and confidence in, the offender's rehabilitation.
2. The prison employee's concern is most effectively manifested by gestures of interest and acts of assistance for the offender which exceed the minimal requirements of the employee's job in the prison.

Staff reformative influences on criminals involve a change in the offender's perception of his relationship to others in our society. These men, previously treated as though members of an untouchable caste, were accepted in prison as a matter of course, in long periods of daily contact, by persons who were secure and content in a respected social status. Gradually this seems to have given the offenders the habit of identifying themselves with persons in these legitimate and conventional statuses, rather than thinking of themselves as in a distinct criminal group rejected by the noncriminal world. Each favorable experience seems to enhance an offender's ability to overcome whatever obstacles he may later encounter.

An interpretation of the findings of the sharp contrast between the relatively great impact of some work supervisors on inmates and the lesser influence of caseworkers suggest that the work supervisor's continuous, and close contact with inmates in cooperative tasks placed him in the best position to develop personal relationships with the inmates. The fact that the education and social-class background of inmates generally is closer to that of the work supervisors than to that of the caseworkers also gives the work supervisors an advantage; most caseworkers have a master's degree, but work supervisors usually have little or no college education. Furthermore, each work supervisor normally is employed all day with a small number of inmates, but the caseworker deals with several hundred inmates, averaging only a few contacts per year with each. Therefore, the work supervisor usually is the staff member who can most extensively demonstrate sincere and sustained concern and confidence in the offender's rehabilitation.

The number of inmates per caseworker varies in each prison, but all have exceedingly high casework loads. So that the caseworkers in a large prison may better know the social environment in which his clients live, Glaser makes the following suggestions[4]:

1. Assignment of all inmates in particular work or housing units of a prison as the caseload of a single caseworker so that he might readily know an inmate's experience in prison through acquaintance with the inmate's social environment.
2. Classification of inmates by subcommittees dealing only with men assigned to a limited segment of the prison and including as members the line staff in direct contact with the inmates to be classified.
3. Revision of casework reports to make their preparation less time-consuming, their recording of objective information more concise and standardized, and their reporting on the inmate's prison experience more adequately grounded on observations of the inmate's conduct outside of the caseworker's office.

THE ROLE OF MALE PERSONNEL

A study[5] was made to explore and attempt to determine the extent to which male personnel employed by women's prisons can help women inmates to gain a more appropriate perspective of themselves in relation to their future participation as members of society.

With role-confused women in prison from having come in conflict with authority, it is important to reshape their self-concept in order that they may reidentify themselves with the feminine role.

The most numerous and severe problems which were evident

---

[4] *Ibid.*, p. 211.

[5] Eyman, Joy S.: *The Role of Male Personnel In A Women's Prison.* (Unpublished Master's thesis, Florida State University, Graduate School, Gainesville, 1964.)

throughout a study made of the psychological needs of women in a correctional institution had to do with the individual herself, and they involved such things as the psychologist has referred to as self-acceptance, self-understanding, and self-realization.

It is the opinion of Cassel and Van Vorst[6] that the immediate family unit is more an inextricable part of the adult female than it is of the male, and that when she is separated from that unit through commitment to a correctional institution, the problems in this area are quite acute. The opinions of inmates involved in this study rated the family adjustment problems as being only second to that of the personal and self-adjustment of the individual.

Barbara Kay[7] states that the socialization tests on the reformatory inmates definitely show that there is no use proceeding on the assumption that women inmates are angels as compared to men. The staff will have to work just as hard to upgrade women offenders as the staff at a men's institution. This means that there must be really effective measures of reeducation of the inmate through the auspices of every staff member with whom inmates have contact.

If we can somehow change the way in which the inmate views herself while we have her in the reformatory, she will have a much better opportunity for good social adjustment when she is returned to society.

An article, "Educational Preparation For The Female Role,"[8] states that we must realize that men and women are not the same, although they are equal. Both male and female should be given the opportunity to develop themselves to their fullest capabilities. One of the major goals of women should be the fulfillment of her biological maternal role: not merely reproduc-

[6] Cassel, Russell N., and Van Vorst, Robert B.: Psychological needs of women in a correctional institution. *American Journal of Correction,* January-February, 1961, pp. 22-24.

[7] Kay, Barbara A.: Female prisoners; their concepts of self. *Police,* November-December, 1962, p. 41.

[8] Lipman, Aaron: Educational preparation for the female role. *The Journal of Educational Society,* September, 1959, pp. 40-43.

tion, but more importantly, caring for and molding the development of the child.

Educators must help women understand that the homemaker's maternal role calls for knowledge and expertness as does any other occupational role. Emphasis on this role does not imply the elimination or denigration of cultural and occupational creativity for women; it is merely adding another dimension, that of physiological fulfillment. Many directors of state correctional systems (all of whom are male) use the "father-image" as their excuse to appoint a male to be the superintendent of a women's institution. To me this is a complete fallacy. I have come to the conclusion that the father-image as an image of constant and unfailing strength is a product of male sociologists, male psychologists, male psychiatrists, and just plain males—and that we females have been gullible enough to accept this image as being a valid concept.

My conclusion is that the father-image does not remain constant for a female, as is the case for a male. For example, when a grown male thinks of the father-image, he sees it unchanged throughout his life: an image of strength. As a small boy, he was loved and protected by his father. His father represented a pillar of strength to be adored and emulated. As the boy grew older, his father remained strong, forcing him to accept responsibility and thus to become a man of strength. To illustrate—rather than give his son an advance on his allowance, the father makes the son earn the money through extra chores at home.

When a grown female thinks of the father-image, she sees the image of her childhood—the same one of love and protection and strength that her brother sees. As a small girl she ran crying to her father, where she was sheltered in his arms until she was no longer afraid. His physical strength always protected her and quieted her sobs from pain or imaginary fears. It quieted as well her outraged cries of fear of her brothers—after she had provoked them to the limit and when she should have been punished instead of protected. This is the father-image of unfailing strength that the grown female sees.

But this is the image that does not remain constant, as is

the case for the male. Another father-image, the image which was held by the female during her teen-age years, is also very real. This is an image that can be manipulated. Still strong when or if she wishes but also weak—putty in her hands, to be used as she has learned throughout her years of unconscious study of her father. To illustrate—the teen-age daughter goes to her father for some extra money "for a beautiful dress" that she knows he will "just love." And her allowance "won't *quite* cover" the cost of the dress. So her father *gives* her the extra money—which amounts to roughly twice her total allowance.

In young womanhood, a third image of the male appears— that of lover as well as protector. Here the female not only is dependent upon the male, but also uses all of her feminine wiles of manipulation on him. The success of the relationship depends upon her subtlety in that the male must believe he is the pillar of strength throughout.

In middle life, still another image of the male is evident. The female becomes the protector of her young, yet retains the relationship of the third image or that of lover and protector.

It is only in the female's declining years, years of returned dependency, that the father-image of her childhood, one of unfailing strength, returns, and with it this psychological need for the father-protector.

In working with women in corrections, these different father-images must be considered. To most women in prison, a male superintendent as the father-image is the image of the female teen-ager, wife, and young mother—all images to be manipulated. It is only the very old female inmate (and these are extremely few) who regards a male superintendent as a father-image of strength.

Unquestionably, the father-image of strength and authority *should* be present in all female institutions (although extremely few women inmates have ever known this image during child-hood), but this image can best be portrayed by other than the superintendent. Male guards are the best source for this father figure, for they represent strength through physical protection (as Marshall Dillon of Dodge City does in the television series *Gunsmoke*).

Other male personnel, such as business managers, teachers,

and farm managers, contribute to what sociologist Charles H. Cooley calls "the looking-glass image." This phenomenon, the tendency to adjust our conduct to the conduct of others toward us, is a central factor in personality. This is evident from the fact that the character and weight of that other person in whose mind we see ourselves make all the difference in our feelings. We are ashamed to seem evasive in the presence of a brave one, gross in the eyes of a refined one, and so on. These other males must personify the male role so that the women in prison may respect it and be comfortable in assuming a feminine role.

The female offender can only be understood in the context of her social role as determined by her constitutional differences, her psychological differences, and her social position, all of which are interrelated.

Females in their youth are daughters and sisters. In adulthood, they assume their identification of wives and mothers. At each level, their behavior is expected to coincide with these established roles. The family remains our basic unit, with the male member being charged with the responsibility of assuring its economic security. A woman's role is that of a homemaker dependent upon her husband. In our present-day culture, it is acceptable for women to combine marriage and careers. However, it is not acceptable for the working mother to neglect her child or children in favor of a job. She must be capable of discharging both responsibilities in good fashion.

Since in our male-dominated culture it is supposedly the male who selects his help-mate to establish his family unit, the girl is groomed to be sexually attractive so that she is chosen in the first place. Sexual attractiveness, however, is not to be considered synonymous with sexual accessibility. Our mores dictate what amounts to a double standard for sexual behavior. Regardless of indications to the contrary, the reputation for chastity is still an important criterion of marriageability and acceptability as a social equal in respectable society. Once married, a woman is presumed to spend most of her life in devotion and service to her husband and family. She is expected to be faithful to her husband. If *he* is not, he usually finds understanding, as the wife will be inclined to assume the responsibility of having been derelict in her duties.

In all his roles, aggressiveness of the male is accepted. The female, who must assume the less overt role, must operate more subtly and less directly. If she does not, she is likely to be called by any number of unflattering names. So, having no alternative, it is not above her principles to connive or manipulate in order to get her wishes satisfied and achieve her goals.

Since a law-abiding female's goal is a happy and successful marriage, it would appear that her status, security, response, and acceptability of her self-image as a woman must depend upon the establishment of satisfactory relationships with the other sex. This same situation prevails with the female offender—both are women! Any woman's driving motivations, accordingly, tend to be emotional. Her major aim is emotional security, as her principal satisfactions are measured by the nonmaterial values of love, affection, and service to her family.

If a woman reverts to prostitution, becomes involved in thefts or forgeries, or neglects her children, she has made a mockery of our concept of her role. This defiance, accordingly, is considered not only unconventional but "bad." When boys or men become involved in legal difficulty, some understanding and acceptance may be shown them by their families, neighbors, and employers. This is not the case with antisocial girls and women. Again, the double standard of conduct is operating.

Unfortunately, there are also men in corrections who are influenced by the double standard. Some men are too punitive toward women in trouble, while others go to the opposite extreme; police, judges, and juries are at times too lenient with women only *because* they are women. This is especially true if the offender is the mother of small children. Women who commit such offenses as shoplifting, burglary, petty larceny, and public intoxication evoke sympathy in male authorities and get special consideration as a result. Women are seldom arrested or prosecuted for homosexual activities or for submitting to criminal abortions, though these are law violations. Where other sorts of crime are concerned—particularly in cases of prostitution —the woman is arrested and brought into court, although her male counterpart is not even taken into custody. This inconsistent treatment poses a particular problem when women officers have to work with male supervisors and male judges whose knowledge of the problem is limited. In fact, obtaining consistent decisions and approval for effective treatment for female offenders is difficult.

With a double standard of conduct operating for men and women, neither sex can be entirely objective toward the opposite sex. Obtaining consistent decisions and approval for effective treatment for female offenders is extremely difficult when the superintendent is a male. Because they best understand female psychology, the leadership of a women's institution should be in the hands of a competent woman superintendent, of professional stature, with a working knowledge of the behavioral sciences.

SUMMARY

Quality of staff is the most important factor in a women's institution. The success of the institution depends primarily upon the personnel. Because of the close contact between inmates and staff, it is necessary to identify and remove any staff member who is detrimental to the goals of the program.

Glaser has made a study which reveals the magnitude of the effect the staff has upon inmates. He has found that if the staff is to compete successfully with the criminal associates of an inmate and inspire anticriminal values, being liked certainly is a major staff asset, although not a guarantee of success.

A necessary condition, if not alone sufficient, for a staff member's favorable influence upon an inmate appears to be the capacity to treat the inmate pleasantly. The most frequently cited type of reason for disliking an officer was his manner of expressing himself toward inmates rather than specific things he did. Staff influence on inmates varies directly with staff showing the inmate the same type of personal behavior that causes a man to be liked or disliked in nonprison relationships.

It was found that the officers whom the men credited as having been rehabilitative influences gave the inmates self-respect. The officers were frank, fair, and considerate.

It is impressive in the Glaser study how often the inmate's regard and respect for the officer was cemented by the officer's maintaining the same attitude and availability to the inmate outside of prison as in.

Some state prisons maintain strict nonfraternization rules for fear the staff will be induced to commit illegal acts. Prison security seems aided not so much by nonfraternization rules as by the staff's inculcation with the goals of the prison service, with moral responsibility, and with sufficient sophistication regarding criminal machination to prevent their being "conned" too readily.

Custodial officers can be said to have the greatest total impact everywhere. This suggests the significance of their job in terms of potential for favorable or unfavorable influence.

The "treatment personnel" had the distinction of being least infrequently the most disliked, but their relatively low frequency of selection for either the liked or disliked designation suggests that these personnel have less total impact on inmates than might be expected from the emphasis on treatment as the main function of these modern prisons.

Prison staff could easily achieve a much greater influence on a larger proportion of inmates using these principles:

1. The prison employee who has the greatest reformative influence on an offender is the one who is able to demonstrate sincere and sustained concern for and confidence in the offender's rehabilitation.
2. The prison employee's concern is most effectively manifested by gestures of interest and acts of assistance for the offender which exceed the minimal requirements of the employee's job in the prison.

Male personnel in women's prisons are most desirable, but not as the superintendent. Male guards depict the father-image of strength and authority. Other male personnel contribute to Cooley's "looking-glass image." This phenomenon, the tendency to adjust our conduct to the conduct of others toward us, is a central factor in personality.

Because they best understand female psychology, the leadership of a women's institution should be in the hands of a competent woman superintendent, of professional stature, with a working knowledge of the behavioral sciences.

BIBLIOGRAPHY

Books

American Correctional Association: *Directory of State and Federal Correctional Institutions.* New York, American Correctional Association, 1963.

————: *Manual of Correctional Standards.* New York, American Correctional Association, 1954.

Barnes, Harry Elmer, and Teeters, Negley K.: *New Horizons in Criminology.* Englewood Cliffs, Prentice-Hall, 1959.

Bryan, Helen: *Inside.* Boston, Houghton, 1953.

Coleman, James C.: *Abnormal Psychology and Modern Life.* Chicago, Scott, Foresman, 1956.

Glaser, Daniel: *The Effectiveness of a Prison and Parole System.* New York, Bobbs-Merrill, 1964.

Harris, Mary B.: *I Knew Them in Prison.* New York, Viking, 1936.

Higgins, Lois Lundell: *Policewoman's Manual.* Springfield, Thomas, 1961.

Kardiner, Abram: *Sex and Morality.* Indianapolis, Bobbs-Merrill, 1954.

Lekkerkerker, Eugenia C.: *Reformatories for Women in the United States.* The Hague, J. B. Wolters, 1931.

Linder, Robert M.: *Stone Walls and Men.* New York, Odyssey, 1946.

Mead, Margaret: *Male and Female.* New York, William Morrow, 1949.

Monahan, Florence: *Women in Crime.* New York, Ives Washburn, 1941.

Neese, Robert: *Prison Exposures.* Philadelphia, Chilton, 1959.

O'Brien, Edna V.: *So I Went to Prison.* New York, Stokes, 1938.

O'Hare, Kate Richards: *In Prison.* New York, Knopf, 1923.

Pollak, Otto: *The Criminality of Women.* Philadelphia, U. of P., 1950.

Rees, J. Tudor, and Usill, Harley V. (Eds.): *They Stand Apart.* New York, Macmillan, 1955.

Rowles, Burton J.: *The Lady at Box 99.* Greenwich, Seabury, 1962.

Scudder, Kenyon J.: *Prisoners Are People.* Garden City, Doubleday, 1952.

Seward, Georgene H.: *Sex and the Social Order.* New York, McGraw-Hill, 1946.

Smith, G. Milton: *A Simplified Guide to Statistics for Psychology and Education.* New York, Rinehart, 1946.

Sullivan, Katherine: *Girls on Parole.* Boston, Houghton Mifflin, 1956.

Sykes, Gresham M.: *The Society of Captives.* Princeton, Princeton University, 1958.

Tappan, Paul W. (Ed.): *Contemporary Correction.* New York, McGraw-Hill, 1951.

Weidensall, Jean: *The Mentality of the Criminal Women.* Baltimore, Warwick and York, 1916.

Articles and Periodicals

Additon, Henrietta: Institutional treatment of women offenders. *NPPA Journal*, January, 1957, pp. 21-30.

Cassel, Russell N., and Van Vorst, Robert B.: Psychological needs of women in a correctional institution. *American Journal of Correction*, January-February, 1961, pp. 22-24.

Clemmer, Donald: Some apsects of sexual behavior in the prison community. *Proceedings of the Eighty-eighth Annual Congress of Correction of the American Correctional Association.* Detroit, Michigan, 1958.

Cunningham, Gloria: Supervision of the fmale offender. *Federal Probation*, December, 1963, pp. 12-16.

Eyman, Joy S.: The myth of the father-image in women's prisons. *American Journal of Correction*, March-April, 1966, pp. 10-11.

Kay, Barbara: Female prisoners; their concepts of self. *Police*, November-December, 1962, pp. 39-40, 70.

Kellogg, Virginia: Inside women's prison. *Collier's*, June 3, 1950, pp. 15, 37, 40-41.

Lipman, Aaron: Educational preparation for the female role. *The Journal of Educational Sociology*, September, 1959, pp. 40-43.

Lorimer, Annie Elizabeth, and Heads, Marjorie: The significance of morale in a female penal institution. *Federal Probation*, December, 1962, pp. 38-44.

O'Connell, Genevieve: Casework with the female probationer. *NPPA Journal*, January, 1957, pp. 13-20.

Papanek, Ernst: The role of reward and punishment in education and correction. *Federal Probation*, June, 1958, pp. 41-46.

Payak, Bertha J.: Understanding the female offender. *Federal Probation*, December, 1963, pp. 7-12.

Peirce, F. J.: Social group work in a women's prison. *Federal Probation*, December, 1963, pp. 37-43.

Rappaport, Mazie F.: The psychology of the female offender. *NPPA Journal*, January, 1957, pp. 7-12.

Reckless, Walter C.: Female criminality. *NPPA Journal*, January, 1957, pp. 1-6.

Rudensky, Red: This side of the wall. *Federal Probation*, September, 1958, pp. 40-42.

Teachout, Margaret A.: Problems of women parolees. *NPPA Journal*, January, 1957, pp. 31-38.

Williams, Lorraine O'Donnell: Short-term treatment of women: an experiment. *Federal Probation*, September, 1957, pp. 42-51.

Unpublished Material

Eyman, Joy S.: The Role of Male Personnel in a Women's Prison. Unpublished Master's thesis, Graduate School, Florida State University, Graduate School, Gainesville, 1966.

New York State Department of Mental Health: Report on study of 102 sex offenders at Sing Sing Prison. Albany, N. Y., March, 1950.

Stein, Walter: The Effects of Coeducational Activities on Juvenile Institutional Programs. Unpublished Master's thesis, Florida State University Graduate, School, Gainesville, 1963.

Chapter 3

EDUCATION

HISTORY

AT THE TURN of the century, education in prisons was practically unknown. Wardens, in self-righteous agreement with the more or less law-abiding majority, frowned on "coddling" their charges.

Prison education had its beginnings when chaplains found that between a third and half of the prisoners to whom they gave Bibles could not read. Some of the chaplains began teaching reading and writing for purely religious reasons.

A research study[1] of fourteen hundred inmates received at the Reception Center in New York State revealed that 33 percent were functionally illiterate; that is, they scored below the fifth grade on standardized tests. It is not surprising that the percentage of illiteracy among inmates is three times greater than in the general population, since commitments to correctional institutions are largely from the deprived, the school dropouts, the poorly conditioned, the migrant laborers, and those with a lust for roving without worthy objectives.

Of the men and women committed to federal prisons, no less than 96 percent are school dropouts.[2]

ACADEMIC EDUCATION

A study made by Glaser[3] has shown that students in the schools of poorer neighborhoods, who predominate in our cor-

---

[1] Chenault, Price: Correctional institutions helping the functionally illiterate. *ALA Bulletin*, October, 1964, p. 804.

[2] A case of civilized penology, *Nation*, January 31, 1966, p. 115.

[3] Glaser, Daniel: *The Effectiveness of A Prison and Parole System*. New York, Bobbs-Merrill, 1964.

rectional populations, tend to have a background from early childhood of feeling that others are hostile and unappreciative toward them and that they have to be hostile in response. These characteristics tend to be most pronounced among our prisoners, since they so frequently were the most maladjusted even in schools which in entirety tended to be much less conducive to academic pursuits than were schools in average or higher-income areas.

The public has become more aware of this cumulative problem in students from so-called "culturally deprived" settings, and there has been widespread experimentation with special methods of instruction to give such students a sense of acceptance and success in their schooling. The problem is to make studying a more rewarding and exciting activity for them.

Reading-ability deficiency seems to be the key problem with the types of pupil predominant in prison. It is this deficiency which increasingly differentiates those who complete high school from those who drop out, as well as those who progress in college from those who never enter or who enter but fail to remain long.

Perhaps the best-known approach to this problem is that of *programmed learning.* By breaking instruction into bits, in well-planned sequences, programmed texts or teaching machines start students with learning tasks that they can master with ease. The programs also permit students to advance to more difficult tasks only when they have mastered the prerequisite learning. Thus students from the backgrounds which distinguish the correctional population have much more experience with success when studying by programmed methods than most of them encounter with conventional teaching and studying procedures.

It is especially significant in prison to have each individual progress at his own rate, because inmates come to school at all times of the year and with a great variety of prior curriculum exposure and mastery. If all are given the same lessons at the same time, even in classes that have been grouped as well as possible by prior school record or by test scores, parts of each lesson will be frustrating to some students and boring to others. Poor students or students that are easily distraught with schooling tend to do distinctly better with programmed instruction than with conventional teaching.[4]

Besides the need to increase the challenge of prison education is the need to alter the social experience which offenders have associated with schooling. Her personal relationships with teachers have frequently been characterized by conflict. By contrast, her most rewarding social experience has often been among peers who share her problems and who extol her hostility to school authorities.

One of the needs of the student who has felt persistent failure in school is a need to feel that she is regarded as personally important and to feel that she is well liked. A person who is of value to herself gives herself the best care, treatment, protection, and training possible, thereby enhancing her value to herself and to others. In this area, the staff of the prison can be of great help by not making the inmate feel degraded, even though she is or has been. Inmates should consistently be reminded of their personal value, both to themselves and to others.

Most inmates have some admirable qualities, although quite often these qualities are misapplied (i.e. loyalty to the wrong person or ideas). Redirection of these qualities can make them real assets to the inmate, rather than liabilities. Inmates fail in their rationalizations to recognize that all inmates have one thing in common: their moral codes are not acceptable to society, no matter what particular ingredient is lacking.

Many prison-school pupils come from a school background of "social promotions." They are not retarded in grade completed but are revealed by test to have an educational achievement grossly below that for the grade in which they were last registered. They are used to school being a place where one "gets by" without any real effort and regardless of whether or not learning occurs. They come from a background of boredom in school to a situation where schooling, if it were suddenly to be as demanding as their prior grade warrants, would be most frustrating.

Realization of this deficiency can be most humiliating, and

---

[4] Glaser, Daniel: The effectiveness of correctional education. *American Journal of Correction*, March-April, 1966, p. 5.

resistance to school will be evoked if they are placed in a grade well below that which they thought they had achieved. Yet studies which begin at a point where their knowledge stops may be essential. Resulting ego shock can be reduced by avoidance of grade designation; to falsify grade levels by exaggerating them is to assure future ego shock from failure.

One corruption in prison schooling results when prison schools play the social promotion game or at least when they maintain the atmosphere of social-promotion slum schools. By not caring whether or not the students learn or even whether the classroom discussions are perpetually bull sessions irrelevant to the subject matter of the course, some prison education directors make their lives extremely soft. The inmates who have found such a school an easy way to do time will see to it that the school looks like a constructive enterprise; they will make impressive charts on inmate participation in school. These are places where the teachers merely serve time along with their students.

Other kinds of corruption in prison schooling are stimulated by the fact that most correctional systems let their inmates know that participation in prison school will be rewarded. Incentive systems motivate the inmate to use her time constructively, but they also motivate many inmates to try to convey a fraudulent impression of school achievement.

In prison, cheating takes many forms. Copies are made of correspondence course lessons and are sold for cigarettes or other commissary goods. Sometimes a bright inmate will complete a whole course for another inmate for a carton or two. Clerks in the prison school and inmate teachers can be pressured or bribed to falsify records of course completion or, minimally, to check examination papers before they are graded officially. Wherever this sort of thing can occur, you are dealing with a lazy prison school administration.

If the staff will insist on supervising all final or other key examinations themselves, if they will base course credit primarily on such examinations, and if they will keep the records of major examinations and course completions entirely and continuously under their control, inaccessible to any inmate, a report on an inmate's educational achievement in prison will be dependable.

Wherever inmates are involved in key examination supervision or have access to key school records, corruption in prison education is not just an ever-present danger—it probably is a usually present reality for some fraction of the inmates.

Research is the key to progress. In correctional education (both academic and vocational), there is not enough research literature available to meet the needs of prison schools. In addition, each correctional system has unique features in sentencing and parole policies and in the communities it serves, which make some of the knowledge it needs apply only to it. Procurement of this knowledge requires two kinds of research.

The first research need is follow-up data, on a routine basis, regarding the utilization of prison schooling in postrelease life and regarding its correlation with nonrecidivism. Parole-supervision agents should routinely determine whether a parolee is working and what kind of work she is doing. They could routinely record this on forms on which they could also note the parolee's response to inquiry on what prison training she is using at her job. If these forms were sent back to prison, there would be a basis for evaluating the practical impact of much specific training, as well as correlating the relationship between prison education participation or progress and postrelease self-sufficiency.

For those releasees who do not receive parole or when a follow-up is desired on criminality beyond the parole period, a partially satisfactory substitute is the record on releasees returned to prison within the same state during a particular postrelease period. This can be supplemented by the record on inquires from those states which routinely request information on prior prison record when they incarcerate someone who previously served time elsewhere.

The second type of research need is experimental research. It is valuable both for measuring the effectiveness of a new correctional education enterprise and procuring financial support for new enterprises.

Experimental research is more conclusive than other research, but its findings still are not absolute and final. Sometimes the impact of a program comes from some unintended feature of it rather than from the apparent features; it may be due only to the unusual personalities of the officials which the program employs or to the unusual enthusiasm or caution distinguishing the administration of a new program. Only as experiments are repeated in different settings and circumstances and the results are consistent can we gain extreme certainty about the validity of its findings.

Where support of a new program is not readily forthcoming because of doubts as to whether it is worthwhile, this resistance will generally be reduced markedly should one propose that the program be introduced only on a controlled experimental basis.

G.E.D. Testing

The General Educational Development (G.E.D.) Testing program, whereby inmates are given the opportunity to earn a certificate of high school equivalency, should become an important part of every prison academic educational program. Every woman who is fortunate enough to pass the tests experiences a boost in morale, an improved self-image, and an increased confidence that may be more beneficial than anything else the institution may do for her.

Those enrolling in the G.E.D. program should be given the following tests: the Iowa Test of Basic Skills (1958), the Gates Reading Survey (1958), the Stanford Achievement Tests (1953), and the Shipley-Hartford Intelligence Test (1946). A correlation has been made between achievement and IQ Scores and the G.E.D. Scores.[5] The Gates Reading Survey proved to be the best predictor of success. A minimum score of 11.0 grade reading level on the Gates test proved almost imperative to pass the G.E.D. tests. Stanford arithmetic subtests 5 and 6 with a minimum grade of 9 and spelling subtest 3 and language subtest 4 with a minimum grade level of 8 also proved to be excellent indicators of success. These correlations not only predict when a candidate is ready for the test but also indicate in which areas the candidate needs tutoring.

---

[5] Blank, Lucile E.: Education in a short-term institution. *American Journal of Correction*, November-December, 1966, p. 22.

The G.E.D. Test consists of five two-hour tests. Test One measures ability to use correct and effective English in written expression. Tests two, three, and four measure ability to read, understand, and interpret material in social studies, natural science, and literature, respectively. Test five measures ability to solve problems in mathematics.

LIBRARY SERVICES

History

In 1840, a library was established in Sing Sing Prison and directed by the prison chaplain. When the state administration changed, the library was abolished in 1843. Ten years later, the Board of Inspectors recommended that it be reopened, and in 1855 an appropriation of two hundred dollars was made for that purpose.

At the meeting of the American Library Association in Chicago in 1912, it was strongly recommended that an ALA representative attend the annual meetings of the American Prison Association to urge the establishment of institution libraries.

Librarian's Role

The librarian needs to see herself in a somewhat different role in institution literacy education. There is little the librarian can do, particularly with the very beginners, except as she works with and through the classroom teachers. The following are several ways in which the librarian may assist.

1. Make the library truly a repository for the best and most up-to-date literature in the field of literacy education.
2. Acquire an understanding of the nature and characteristics of the inmate population so that reading matter may be made available for meeting the needs, interests, and abilities of those confined.
3. In cooperation with the teachers of literacy education and other institution authorities, make the library a depository for the various kinds of communications media so that they will be readily available.
4. Become informed about the courses of study and be alert for

new and up-to-date instructional materials and programs which may be referred to the teachers for review.

5. Maintain an up-to-date promotional program which will keep both staff and inmates appraised of what is in the library.
6. Convey to the teachers the techniques of personalized individual approaches to the learning processes which experienced librarians use so effectively.
7. Make available programmed courses of instruction for examination by teachers.

The regrettable dearth of material for the low-level reader places an added responsibility on the librarian. She must be able to illustrate ways in which higher-level books can be used, by selecting that portion which meets a present reading level and by stressing its probable value in motivating the reader to grow in reading accomplishment.

For example, the illiterate inmate can "read" a book with many photographs and drawings without difficulty, but the book's value does not stop there. Through formal study or guidance from a teacher she can learn to read the words. The ultimate result is a well-used book in the hands of a more mature reader.

As inmates move toward the functional literate level, the librarian can perform increasingly the same services for these as she does for the avid reader.

Service to staff personnel includes using the physical area of the library. Art shows, planned to motivate the illiterate viewer to a desire for reading, may be arranged. This can be through a display of artists' biographies coordinated with a selected theme, such as the achievement of artists who have overcome the handicap of physical disability, environment, or economic or social strata. One federal institution motivates the functional illiterate by the combined use of books and music. During the weekly music appreciation class, the librarian introduces and discusses appropriate books displayed in the listening area.

The library is a very important bridge to the outside world to which the inmate will one day return. By reading, the inmate keeps herself abreast of local, national, and international affairs. Through the library, she is able to keep in touch with people, changing customs, business methods, and social and civic problems that she would not ordinarily come in contact with in the usual prison environment.

The skillful teacher, with library resources at hand, will give attention to other aspects of inmate development while she is teaching reading. The inmates will read elementary occupational books, listen to recordings, view films, and engage in occupational discussions. Likewise, a program designed to help the individual understand her problems related to the home, the community, work, and herself will be provided. Becoming a reader is not an end in itself.

Perhaps one of the more significant services that institution libraries can provide in the years ahead would be studies resulting from the federal program against poverty. Both inmates and staff of correctional institutions are aware of the need for education. The institution library can accent the feeling by dissemination of appropriate information.

Low-Budget and No-Budget Libraries

Not all women's institutions will be fortunate enough to have a full-time professional library staff or an adequate book budget. Therefore, the work done by the Library Association of Portland[6] is brought to your attention.

The request by the sheriff for a library at the new correctional unit posed a problem in time for the Bookmobile. The only solution seemed to be the deposit of a fairly large collection of books at the institutions, which would be manned by inmate help.

Bookshelves were discarded units from a nearby college which was remodeling. Room was found in one of the new dormitories, with half, a space about 25 feet by 45 feet, becoming the library and the other half designated for use as a chapel. Lighting, intended for a dormitory, was inadequate at night time when the library was heavily used. Therefore, lighting had to be made stronger.

In the maximum security jail, where space was a problem because any library had to be located so that it could be moni-

---

[6] Kling, Joseph: Books behind bars. *Library Journal,* April 1, 1967, pp. 1424-1425.

tored by one of the guards, a well-lighted mop-and-broom closet, 12 by 14 feet, was turned into the library. When shelving was built on three sides of the room, this small area would hold 3,000 books.

To find books to fill the shelves, official discards were used, along with gift books presented to the library, duplicates no longer needed from the Extension and Bookmobile collections, and other gleanings. Reference books came from a subbranch that had been closed.

Old easy chairs were begged from friends, who also furnished ash trays, pictures, and flowers.

When access to the library became a problem for some inmates, a hospital cart came into use, with the library assistant trustee pushing it around to the cells several times a week.

To make the main body of the book collection available to everyone, a book catalog, with author, title, and subject entries for each book was printed. The catalog, which is revised once a year, is available on the book cart and in all cell blocks.

Attempt should be made to have books of interest for as many inmates as possible. There should be about five hundred books which are basic to any library. The reference books may be a year or two behind those of the public library, since they may be inherited when the new edition is brought out. The same would be true of encyclopedias.

This type of book service requires very little time of the city libraries' professional help. In Portland, only four hours of staff time a week is given to service several jails, and no other time or money is expended by the public library.

Job application forms can be secured from a local firm and they could be used in practicing reading and writing. In math, an income tax form or a newspaper ad about buying a car on time can provide practical examples to illustrate a point. Every effort should be made to keep the inmate's interest and to provide her with practical skills which she can use upon release.

To give the teacher some idea of the actual educational level of the inmate, Stanford Achievement Tests or Jaztac Tests should be administered. The Jaztac Test is easier to administer, takes less time to complete, and yields sufficiently accurate results to warrant its use.

Hooked on Books

The Program

To "deviate from the norm" is not unheard of in prisons. Therefore, I would make this suggestion to both the institutional teachers and the librarians—to deviate from the normal procedure of teaching and libraries and follow the suggestions made in *Hooked On Books.*[7]

Briefly, "English In Every Classroom" is an approach to learning based on the dual concepts of *Saturation and Diffusion.* The first of these key concepts, saturation, proposed to so surround the student with newspapers, magazines, and paperbound books that she comes to perceive them as pleasurable means to necessary ends. The advantages inherent in selecting such materials for classroom use are very great. First and most important, all newspapers, most magazines, and the great majority of paperbound books are written in the knowledge that commercial disaster is the reward for creating paragraphs that people *should* read. With the choice a clear one between market success and business failure, publishers, editors and writers know that survival depends on producing words that people *will* read. This program advances the radical notion that inmates are people and should be treated accordingly.

A second and perhaps equally important advantage in saturating the inmate's environment with newspapers, magazines, and paperbound books is their relationship to the world outside the prison.

The third advantage of these materials is closely related to the second. Not only do newspapers, magazines, and paperbound books *enable* the inmate to deal with the world as it is, but they *invite* her to do so.

The fourth and final asset of softbound materials is that they get a very important message across. No matter how bad one feels about her world, she has only to read a newspaper or magazine to know that somebody else has got it worse!

Saturation applies in principle not only to the selection and

---

[7] Fader, Daniel N., and McNeil, Elton B.: *Hooked On Books: Program And Proof.* New York, Berkeley, 1968.

distribution of periodicals and softbound texts throughout the curriculum but to the explosion of writing in the inmate's school environment. The explosion is based upon the practice of diffusion. Whereas saturation refers to the materials used in every classroom to induce the inmate to enter the doorway of literacy, diffusion refers to the responsibility of every teacher in every classroom to make the house of literacy attractive.

In discharging this responsibility, every teacher becomes an intermediary between the inmate and functional literacy. In order that the inmate may come to view writing as a means to an end, all ends which she pursues in a scholastic context must insist upon writing as the means through which they can be approached. In short, every teacher becomes a teacher of English, and English is taught in every classroom.

Writing

Only one method in learning to write can be expected to succeed—the constant practice of writing itself. Though the teacher and her texts are important, the one indispensable element is the continuous prose output of the inmate herself.

Of the many and varied encouragements and inducements to writing within the scope of "English In Every Classroom," none has been more consistently successful than the journal.

In addition to the two paperbound books from the library that each entering inmate student is allowed to choose for her own and the paperbound dictionary she is given to keep, she also receives from her English teacher a spiral notebook. This is identified as her journal, an appropiate name for a notebook intended for daily use by every inmate student. When she is given her journal, the inmate student is told that quantity of production will be the only criterion for judging her writing. Content, style, grammer, rhetoric—all are insignificant compared to quantity. This journal, the inmate student is told, has only one reason for existence: to provide her with a field upon which she can practice her writing.

She will be required to write a minimum number of pages each week (usually two), and she will be asked each Thursday to turn in her journal to the English teacher, who will return it on Friday. The English teacher will read the journal only if she is invited to do so by the inmate. Under no circumstances will the journal be corrected. It will be assessed for quantity, nothing else.

The fact that the journal is never read by teachers, except by specific invitation, allows the inmate to use vituperation and obscenity as methods by which she may free herself from some of the frustration and fear that shackle her to illiteracy.

The quantitative view of writing has as a necessary corollary the permissive handing of journal entries by the teacher. Whether written inside or outside of class, whether legible or barely intelligible, whether a sentence, a paragraph, or a page—each entry is another building block in the structure of the inmate student's literacy. If the teacher can bring herself to regard the journal in this way, she will be equally satisfied with prose that is original and prose that is copied from a newspaper, a magazine, or a book. And both she and her student will be more satisfied with work which is evaluated by no one.

From copying from a newspaper or a magazine or a book, most inmate students go naturally to the next stage of journal usage—the diary. They fill their pages with the thoughts and happenings of their daily life.

If this permissiveness in the nature of the entry is closely coupled with an unvarying weekly check on the amount of production, then the formula for success is much of human enterprise—a little license with accompanying obligation—can make the journal an exceptionally useful teaching tool.

Softbound Library

Prison librarians should take a useful lesson from operators of paperbound bookstores, who have learned to let their merchandise sell itself by arranging their stores so that customers are surrounded by colorful and highly descriptive paper covers.

Where change is most badly needed is in the ideas of economy which dictate the selection of books and methods of display. For what reason other than economy of space are books displayed with their spines out? The spine of a book, with its Dewey decimal notations, is no more attractive than any other spine with such markings would be. And yet we expect the partially literate inmate, who relates to very little through words, to relate to books through words printed on their spines!

This the same inmate who is *always* attracted to pictures, whether found in comic books or on the television screen. Why then not make the most of her tastes and predispositions, give up the false economy which shelves large numbers of unread books, and attract her to books through bright pictures on their covers? Why not replace the typically drab, unread books of prison libraries—libraries full of books with pictureless, unopened covers—with paperbound books that attract inmates by the bright covers that commercial artists and advertising men have made inviting?

What of the expense of purchasing paperbound books to begin with and of maintaining a steady supply to replace the easily tattered, broken, and lost paperback? Books tested in this program are proving to be virtually indestructible—not because they can't easily be ripped or destroyed, but because they have become something of value and are treated accordingly.

If reading activity follows visual appeal as effect follows cause, what about space problems of shelving books with their covers showing? The answer lies in the wall racks and free-standing spinners traditionally used to promote paperback sales in corner drugstores and other places where space is at a premium.

The problem of library space has another interesting solution —the combination classroom and library. A large classroom can be easily adapted to the minimal space requirements of revolving wire racks for paperbound books.

In order to make selection procedures easier in creating the best possible paperback library, *Hooked On Books* has included in its contents a reading list of one thousand paperback books. These have proved to be most popular, and they take into account the interests of girls. Study guides for *West Side Story* and *Anne Frank: The Diary Of A Young Girl* are also included in *Hooked On Books*.

Regarding the library as something less than an irresistible attraction to inmates is a useful first step in revitalizing it. Implicit in this approach is an objective review of its lending

procedures. Instead of placing the responsibility for first acquaintance upon the inmate and/or teacher, the responsibility
should be put where it rightfully belongs—upon the books
themselves. *Give* each inmate a paperbound book or two when
she enters the prison. Let her understand that she may have
any other paperbound book in the library by the simple expedient
of trading a book she has for a book she wants. Then *schedule*
her twice each week for the opportunity of book borrowing.

VOCATIONAL TRAINING OR MAKING A LEGAL LIVING

Why do some ex-inmates fail and others succeed when they
are released from prison? There are many different reasons,
for inmates are by no means one class of people, and they don't
fall into distinct groups.

In the chapter "Variations in Postrelease Success and
Failure,"[8] Dr. Glaser presents a large group of individual case
histories which give a picture of the great range of personalities
that are being discussed. They do have some things in common,
though, such as the following:

1. Ninety percent of major crimes reported in the FBI's Uniform
   Crime Report for the United States involve taking someone else's
   money or property. . . . Hence it is appropriate to say that
   most crime is either a supplement or a substitute for work, as a
   means of procuring an income.
2. In the prison population, both whites and Negroes are pre-
   dominantly unskilled and have dropped out of school early.
3. Employment in prison may be the first steady work experienced
   by most inmates.

The key to "success" after prison, then obviously is finding
a legal way to make a living.

This survey also showed that learning a trade or in other
ways preparing for a better job opportunity outside of prison
was the first interest of most inmates at every prison studied.

Vocational training has been a part of all federal and most
state educational and rehabilitation programs for many years.

---

[8] Glaser, Daniel: *The Effectiveness of A Prison and Parole System.* New
York, Bobbs-Merrill, 1964, pp. 54-85.

However, many prisons have trained their inmates primarily for two purposes: to provide for the needs of the institution itself (providing food services, maintaining grounds and buildings, for example) and to provide for certain specialized needs of the state (making cotton mattresses, for example). It's fair to say, however, that a woman faces heavy odds when she leaves prison and starts looking for a job making cotton mattresses.

Vocational education courses should be set up to train women in occupations for which there is known to be a demand. The object is simply to increase the odds that a woman who is released will be employed and not just be out on the street looking for work or looking for trouble—in other words, to give her something approaching an even break, which is all most of these women want anyway.

Vocational education or occupational training is the best means of helping these women adapt to the process of getting along in the community.

Some Suggestions for Vocational Training Programs

The purpose of vocational training is to provide a special program for selected inmates whose inability to profit from routine training would find them entering the current labor market with severe handicaps. It should be designed to provide those selected with the proper social attitudes, motivation, and skills necessary for gainful employment in occupations in the area to which they are returning.

Before enrollment in certain programs, a committee of prison officials should carefully screen all applications, taking into consideration each woman's tested ability, work experience, education, and attitude.

Because certain vocational program graduates must be licensed by the state before they can practice (beauty culture, for instance), arrangements for accreditation of all schools should be insured before the instigation of such programs. It is sometimes possible to become affiliated with an accredited school in the community. Other cases may require legislative acts.

Although vocational training is geared to the employment needs of the community and state to which the inmate will return, there are certain vocations that are needed thoughout the country and are especially suited to women. Two of these are beauty culture and the paramedical field.

The whole field of data processing now offers jobs for women. Both key punch operators and computer programmers can be taught in women's prisons. Key punch operators need a proficiency in typing, and computer programmers need a mathematical background. Although both courses can be taught without equipment (I.B.M. has a course where no machines are used in the training program, and a computer programmer course could do work for a local company in order to compile and test the programs), the use of equipment is, of course, most desirable. Where machines are rented, bought, or used, a maintenance agreement should be included with them.

Prison Industry as Vocational Training

A prison industry that can produce both money and vocational training is industrial sewing. Skilled power-machine operators are in demand in many areas of the country. Also in this category is the operation of a greenhouse. Floriculture as well as flower arranging can be taught. Garments could be sold to state institutions, and flowers could be provided for state functions.

Dairymen are turning to women to help ease the labor shortage. Those dairymen who have tried women in milking operations are pleased with the results. Women are proving to be better milkers than men and understand the problems of swollen udders, mastitis, and other mammary infections. A dairy at the prison can supply products for the prison, as well as train dairy workers.

In conjunction with the Department of Mental Health, it would be possible to have a cottage for mentally retarded girls on the prison grounds, where inmates might take care of the girls. Besides providing workers for the cottage and training and employment for the inmates, both girls and inmates will benefit from the exchange of tender loving care.

Federal Funding

Funding for occupational training in prisons has been greatly helped through Federal programs. Although authorization for such programs can at times be frustrating, two areas of possible financial assistance for vocational training programs that every women's prison should investigate fully are those offered by the Manpower Development and Training Act of 1962 (MDTA), and the Vocational Rehabilitation Administration's Public Law 89-333, the "Amendments to the Vocational Rehabilitation Act." These amendments enlarge the opportunities for VRA contributions to the correctional field.

Role of Occupational Training

Occupational training is one of the major rehabilitative roles of the correctional institution. Many offenders see it as the only rehabilitative or constructive activity the institution has to offer. Inmates will ask for trade training when they will ask for nothing else. It is therefore an entering wedge to other phases of the program. Many inmates find work in which they are interested, rapidly develop skills, gain self-respect, and gradually begin to think more of a future at that occupation than at criminal activities. In many instances, it is a skill acquired in prison which is responsible for changed attitudes and outlooks.

SOCIAL EDUCATION

Social education is a type of adult education directed toward the problems of living in a modern society—problems which have faced and will, after release, continue to face the inmate. The social case worker is the specialist in this field, although counseling is not restricted to the case worker.

Glaser[9] has found that the most important influence in "reforming" inmates comes from the prison staff. Because the influence of keepers on the kept is so important in rehabilitation, every effort should be made to make relationships between the two groups more informal and less authoritarian.

---

[9] *Ibid.*

Both of these subjects are discussed in detail in other chapters of this book.

SUMMARY

Illiteracy among inmates is three times greater than in the general population. A New York study revealed that one third of the inmates were functionally illiterate. Federal prison studies reveal that 96 percent of the inmates are school dropouts.

Reading-ability deficiency seems to be the key problem with the types of pupil predominant in prison. Perhaps the best approach to this problem would be programmed learning, which breaks instruction into bits, in well-planned sequences. Programmed texts or teaching machines start students with learning tasks that they can master with ease.

The most important teachers to have in prisons are reading specialists. If no other teachers—either academic or vocational—can be hired, some way should be found to secure reading specialists.

An important part of every prison academic educational program should be the General Educational Development (G.E.D.) Testing program.

For library services, the program and methods in the book *Hooked On Books,* by Fader and McNiel, is suggested as the most productive, and probably least expensive, method of obtaining an adequate library that will be used.

The key to "success" after prison is finding a legal way to make a living. Also, learning a trade or in other ways preparing for a better job opportunity outside of prison is the first interest of most inmates. Vocational education courses should be set up to train women in occupations for which there is known to be a demand. Accreditation of all schools should be insured before the instigation of vocational programs.

BIBLIOGRAPHY
Books

Fader, Daniel N., and McNeil, Elton B.: *Hooked On Books: Program and Proof.* New York, Berkeley, 1968.
Giallombardo, Rose: *Society Of Women.* New York, Wiley, 1966.

Glaser, Daniel: *The Effectiveness of a Prison and Parole System.* New York, 1964.

Ward, David A., and Kassebaum, Gene G.: *Women's Prison.* Chicago, Aldine, 1965.

Publications

American Correctional Association: *Manual of Correctional Standards.* Prepared by Committee for Revision of 1959 Manual. New York, The American Correctional Association, 1966.

National Council On Crime And Delinquency: Correction in the United States. *Crime And Delinquency.* January, 1967, pp. 185-206.

National Council On Crime And Delinquency: The female offender. *Crime And Delinquency.* January, 1957.

Periodicals

A case of civilized penology. *Nation,* January 31, 1966, p. 115.

Bennett, James V.: A cool look at 'the crime crisis.' *Harper's Magazine,* April, 1964, pp. 123-127.

Blank, Lucille E.: Education in a short-term institution. *American Journal of Correction,* Nov.-Dec., 1966, pp. 21-23.

Burns, Henry J.: Corrections: past, present, future. *Federal Probation,* June, 1969, pp. 26-30.

Case, John D.: We operate a salvage business—not a junk yard! *Federal Probation,* September, 1966, pp. 30-37.

Chenault, Price: Correctional institutions helping the functionally illiterate. *ALA Bulletin,* October, 1964, pp. 804-809.

Dennes, Lloyd B.: Education in prison. *The New Republic,* September 12, 1964, p. 6.

Eckenrode, C. J.: The librarian plays the central role. *ALA Bulletin,* October, 1964, pp. 810-811.

Glaser, Daniel: The effectiveness of correctional education. *American Journal of Correction,* March-April, 1966, pp. 4-9.

Goldie, Patricia: The patient and the inmate. *ALA Bulletin,* July-August, 1967, pp. 843-844.

Hodge, Raymond C.: The rehabilitation process: a prisoner's point of view. *American Journal of Correction,* March-April, 1964, pp. 12-16.

Kling, Joseph: Books behind bars. *Library Journal,* April 1, 1967, pp. 1424-1425.

Leffler, William J.: On being human in the prison community. *Federal Probation,* June, 1968, pp. 30-32.

Mackenzie, Louise L.: Service to inmates and staff. *ALA Bulletin,* October, 1964, pp. 809-810.

Miller, E. Eugene: Education at Bucks County prison. *American Journal of Correction,* March-April, 1967, pp. 22-25.

Rudensky, Morris: After the stretch. *Harper's Magazine,* April, 1964, pp. 180-182.

Sard, Thomas R.: Chance on the outside. *American Education,* April, 1966, pp. 29-33.

Switzer, Mary E.: Vocational rehabilitation and corrections: a promising partnership. *Federal Probation,* September, 1967, pp. 12-16.

Chapter 4

INMATE HEALTH AND MEDICAL SERVICES

OBJECTIVES AND STANDARDS

T HE OBJECTIVES OF A health and medical services program for prisoners must include the promotion of health, the prevention of disease and disability, the cure or mitigation of disease, and the rehabilitation of the inmate.

The inmate comes into the prison with a conception of herself made possible by certain stable social arrangements in her home world. Upon entrance, she is immediately stripped of the support provided by these arrangements. In the accurate language of some of our oldest total institutions, she begins a series of abasements, degradations, humiliations, and profanations of self. Her self is systematically, if often unintentionally, mortified.[1] Dignity, freedom, and individuality must be maintained by those who provide, as well as those who receive, medical services.

In the prison setting, where freedom of choice for both patient and physician is limited, special attention must be given to the personal relationships between patient and doctor to ensure continuity of service, and to foster the development of the best possible patient-doctor relations. Medical services for inmates must be ever on the alert to recognize and deal constructively with those impediments to patient-physician relationships which may occur in the institutional organization.

Structure of Medical Unit

The medical division of a correctional system should be directed by a suitably qualified physician assigned as medical director, responsible to the director of the correctional system.

---

[1] Goffman, Erving: *Asylums.* Garden City, Doubleday, 1961, p. 14.

The medical director will play a dual role: first, as staff advisor to the director of corrections and second, as the senior medical officer in charge of the medical services of all prisons. The medical director's responsibilities include the recruitment and selection of medical specialists to be used as consultants for all correctional institutions.

The institutional medical services should have a chief medical officer responsible for the administration of the local medical services, reporting to the superintendent of his institution and to the medical director of the system.

Staff

The medical staffing pattern of a given correctional institution should be determined by the health needs of the inmate population and the nature of the health services which are to be provided to personnel. Efficient usage of medical personnel requires that the staff be geared to the population level and commensurate with its needs.

A physician in charge of the medical unit is the ideal. Whether these services are full- or part-time depends upon the size and requirements of the institution. Most women's institutions are too small to require the services of a full-time physician. However, they should have the services of a part-time physician.

In selection of this part-time physician, thought should be given to the needs of the inmate population. In a women's prison, these needs are for a specialist in women's diseases, for the most part. Therefore, it would be well to consider the possibility of hiring a resident or assistant resident in the obstetrical-gynecological services of a nearby hospital. Although their time is limited, they will be able to hold weekly, half-day clinics. They will, of course, be on call for emergencies and for telephone consultations. A weekly half-day clinic should suffice for women's institutions where the population is one hundred or less.

Obstetrics and gynecology residents will be able to care for the routine illnesses found in women's prisons and will have the use of other specialists, through the medical director, when the need arises.

The hospital where the prison doctor is serving his residency should be the one to which the inmates are sent when they need hospitalization of any kind. In this way, the inmates can be under the care of the prison doctor.

While the male role does not permit the giving away to fears and temper tantrums, the female role permits working off frustrations through emotional outlets. One finds more crying and begging for recognition and assistance in a women's prison, but much less physically assaultive behavior. There is more use of passive nonconformity, such as illness, in women's prisons, rather than active nonconformity, such as violence or direct verbal abuse.

Therefore, it is very important in women's prisons to have the same doctor attend the inmates so that he may become acquainted with their case histories. Frequent changing of doctors means that the inmates are able to "con" the doctor out of many unnecessary tranquilizers and other medicines.

Residencies in obstetrics and gynecology last for three years. It is possible to retain the services of the same doctor for this length of time if he becomes the prison doctor at the start of his residency. If the services of the chief resident are preferred, the length of service as chief resident is for a period of one year.

In facilities not in charge of a physician, one registered nurse (R.N.) should be administratively responsible for the department, under the supervision of a part-time physician or consulting physicians.

In the case of very small institutions, the staff is often too small to allow the hiring of even an R.N. Under these circumstances, it is still possible to provide some degree of around-the-clock medical coverage through the use of Licensed Practical Nurses (L.P.N.). If the prison does not have a slot in the table of organization for L.P.N.'s, these trained personnel can be hired as matrons. An L.P.N. matron on each shift will be in charge of the medical unit during her tour of duty. One of these L.P.N. matrons should be designated as administratively responsible for the department.

The person in charge of the medical unit, whether a physician or nurse, should be directly responsible to the superintendent of the institution.

Institution medical staffs should also include dentists and psychologists in sufficient numbers to meet the needs of the inmate population served. Paramedical personnel, including technicians, aides, and clerical staff, must be provided in sufficient numbers to adequately support the assigned professional personnel.

PROBLEMS PECULIAR TO PRISONS

Special attention should be given to the integration of the psychiatric and psychological services into the general medical service to insure that the whole medical staff achieves the best possible understanding of the importance of psychological factors in the management of their patients.

The staff is not dealing with mental defectives, psychotics, or neurotics primarily, but with personality disorders—women with character defects. The typical inmate is a sociopath incapable of social cooperation. She has never let people get close to her. All medical staff should be prepared and trained to care for this type of patient, the psychotic, the epileptic, the disturbed, the alcoholic, and the drug addict, as well as patients who have the more typical illnesses.

In addition to the usual strains of living, prison has some all its own—homosexual pressures, the irritation of restrictive rules, which while necessary, seem like harassment to the inmate; the hostility toward sometimes tactless and indifferent employees, fear of other inmates, receiving a "Dear John" letter from home, the sense of helplessness to assist one's family, which may be in dire need, feelings of guilt and shame, and sexual deprivation.

In states which have an indeterminate-sentence law, such as California, in addition to the above strains, there are three situations in an inmate's life when she fears she will "blow her top" and needs supportive therapy if she is to retain her emotional equilibrium. These are the following[2]:

---

[2] Babcock, Lyndon: Hypnotherapy in the prison setting. *American Journal of Correction*, May-June, 1967, p. 11.

1. Preboard Jitters (the period preceding her board appearance when she becomes apprehensive over the decision to be made by the parole board to give her her parole or ask her to serve more time).
2. Postboard Depression (when she is "shot down" by the board, i.e. must continue to serve more time under her indeterminate sentence).
3. Separation Anxiety (having been given a parole date, fear that she will be unable to "make it" on the street).

Newly assigned medical personnel should be provided with appropriate orientation programs to familiarize them with such problems, as well as with the prison setting and all aspects of the medical-care program in which they are assigned. All staff must be strongly aware of security precautions, particularly in regard to keys and drugs.

Some inmates will attempt to hoard or save up the medication issued to them and take it in increased amounts at a specific time to produce an effect in themselves which is other than that intended by the physician prescribing medication. If given the opportunity, an inmate may attempt to convert the medication to another form, that is, heat a pill on a spoon or over a match; or she may take the medication in a manner not intended by the physician, such as sniffing the powder in a capsule. These are admittedly rare instances, but the possibility exists.

Some inmates, either because they feel they don't need the medication prescribed or because they equate it with punishment will attempt to "get back" at the authorities in the institution or relieve themselves of the actual taking of it by secreting the medication either in their hands, under their tongue, between their teeth and their gums, or some other way, and at the earliest possible opportunity dispose of it.

Inmates may, instead of taking their own medicine, conceal it and trade it. This can be done for the gain inherent in bartering the medication, to gain status with other inmates, or to "get back" at the institutional authority by not taking the medication and doing something with it that they know they shouldn't be doing.

Inmates may attempt to accumulate the medication and take an excessive amount. This presents a problem in that a coma, or even death, can develop from an excessive amount of medication. It may be that an inmate will attempt to hoard her medication in order to produce this effect in herself.

The problem of inmate hoarding, trafficking, or disposing of medication is partially an administrative or custodial problem and partially a counseling problem. In counseling, the inmate must be taught what effect the medicine is intended to produce in her so that she is more likely to use the medication properly and to understand its use. From a custodial or administrative viewpoint, it is necessary to work out a system of administering the medication so that it will be impossible for an inmate to conceal or hoard her medication and which will prevent her from eventually selling it, converting it to another form to use herself, or disposing of it. Unfortunately, the more of such measures that must be carried out and the more stringent they are, the greater is the likelihood that the inmate can equate the taking of medication with punishment or an onerous correctional routine.

FACILITIES AND EQUIPMENT

Women's institutions need not provide elaborate and expensive quarters and equipment for operations if arrangements can be made for surgery and other medical work of major importance to be done at a nearby hospital.

Almost without exception, the smaller women's institutions are located near enough to a facility for men to allow them to draw on the larger institution for some part-time services, such as x-rays and routine laboratory procedures. Surgery and maternity cases confined in the nearby city hospital may return to the women's prison hospital for much of their postoperative and postdelivery care.

Women can usually be sent to the local hospitals for surgery and maternity treatment without guards. However, the institution may come under a great deal of criticism from the newspapers if they allow this.

One method used to absolve the women's institution of possible escapes while the inmate is hospitalized without a guard is to grant the inmate a temporary parole which begins when she enters the hospital and is revoked with her return to the prison. When the inmate is on parole, no guard is necessary, and if she flees during her hospitalization, she will have broken parole rather than escaped from prison. Those inmates to be sent to a hospital without guard must be carefully selected.

Sometimes, around-the-clock supervision needs to be given. With a small custodial staff at the institution, the burden of another post to be covered is often beyond the capabilities of the staff. One solution to this is by hiring private nurses, either R.N.'s or L.P.N.'s, to guard the inmate while she is in the hospital. These nurses must be carefully chosen and taught to be custody conscious. By enlisting the aid of the nurses' organizations in the recruitment of nurses to serve such duty prior to the need, the nurses' register can be contacted when such a nurse-guard is needed.

Institutional medical facilities should contain an adequate outpatient clinic, quarters for the isolation of communicable diseases, and nurseries for the newborn if it is the policy to care for babies in the institution.

Facilities should include security units where emotionally disturbed women can receive temporary care in a secure setting under the supervision of the medical staff.

HEALTH AND MEDICAL SERVICES

Preventive health services should begin with a physical examination of each newly received inmate, including routine chest x-rays and Pap smears. Those inmates who are found to be ill upon admission should be hospitalized for treatment.

As a part of the preventive health program, all new arrivals should receive indicated immunizations and vaccinations. The local county health department can be most helpful in working with the institution on their preventive health program.

Reciprocating arrangements with nearby universities in the areas of teaching, training, and research should be developed whenever possible. Through cooperation with a School of Social Welfare, a women's institution can become a field placement unit, providing social services that might otherwise be prohibitive because of cost. Vocational rehabilitation departments are eligible to help with the rehabilitation of qualified inmates.

Suitable screening programs should be developed to insure that all inmates in need of psychiatric attention are recognized and given indicated treatment. Provision must also be made for the care of those inmates with chronic illnesses such as the cardiacs, tubercular, diabetic, epileptic, and those inmates with chronic mental illness.

Every inmate who has a remedial physical condition should be offered suitable medical treatment or surgical correction, to the end that she will be restored to the fullest measure of health prior to her release from the institution. Disfiguring and disabling defects which might interfere with future employment should receive a high priority in the correctional surgical program.

Pregnant Inmates and Their Babies

A problem unique to women's prisons is that of the pregnant inmate. This is also a controversial problem. The majority of superintendents of women's institutions believe that babies should be delivered in community hospitals and placed directly in the community. However, in some states, delivery occurs at the institution hospital, and nurseries are provided at the institution.

Flexibility should allow for the mother who has only a short period of her sentence left and who is in a position to care for her baby when she returns to the community to care for it in the institution until she leaves.

When a child is to be placed in the community at birth, as most children born to inmates are, care must be taken to do the following:

1. Coordinate all staff efforts in placement of the child.
2. Insure consistence in the planning with an expectant mother.
3. Insure good casework practices in the placement of the child.

Initial planning begins when the pregnant inmate arrives or as soon as the pregnancy is discovered. Unless the child is placed for adoption, casework between the institution and the child-placing agency continues actively throughout the inmate's commitment.

This problem is more thoroughly explored in the chapter "Babies in Prison."

Diabetic Inmates

Correctional administrators and workers should become familiar with the behavior of diabetics who are experiencing insulin reaction or its direct opposite, diabetic coma.[3]

Diabetic coma usually results in known diabetics as a result of withdrawal of insulin or infection and is sometimes aggravated by improper eating. The coma usually develops gradually over a period of many hours or a few days. The symptoms can be deceptively vague. Some of the usual symptoms are flushed, dry skin; drowsiness, fruity breath odor; deep, labored breathing; vomiting, dry tongue, and thirst. If a diabetic coma is suspected, immediate medical attention is mandatory; without treatment, diabetic coma results in death.

The opposite condition, insulin reaction (or "insulin shock," known medically as hypoglycemia), appears more rapidly and is much more common than diabetic coma. Often the first sign is excessive moisture appearing on the face. If at any time the diabetic's system has received more than enough insulin for the existing amount of sugar, his blood sugar level falls too far and an insulin reaction ensues. Diabetics who are taking oral compounds (tablets or pills taken by mouth) may also experience hypoglycemia.

Most reactions are mild. They usually can be attributed to the diabetic's having exercised more than usual (thereby burning an extra amount of sugar) or to her having injected more insulin than her system can manage or to her failure to eat enough food to "use up" her supply of insulin. Reaction can appear so suddenly that the diabetic loses her judgment before she has

---

[3] Peck, Franklin B., Sr.: Some facts about diabetic inmates of correctional institutions. *American Journal of Correction*, March-April, 1962, pp. 22-23.

time to recognize its symptoms and take the necessary (and simple) corrective step: eating or drinking something sweet. Every diabetic who takes insulin should have some form of sugar available at all times.

When reaction is too rapid for the diabetic to be capable of self-help, sugar in some form should be given to her immediately. (In some instances, the treatment may have to be repeated at fifteen to thirty-minute intervals). A lump of table sugar, a glass of fruit juice, a piece of candy, or a soft drink can serve the purpose. If the condition is not corrected, the diabetic may lose consciousness entirely.

If a diabetic becomes unconscious for any reason, the best rule is to call a doctor immediately.

Coma can become a serious or fatal threat to the life of a diabetic inmate if attention is not given to establishing a satisfactory daily balance between her insulin intake, diet, and exercise. All diabetics have an apparent insulin lack in some degree, and diet, for every diabetic, is a fundamental key to control of the condition. Almost half the known diabetics have enough natural insulin to maintain a satisfactory control by diet alone. Others have been able to take pills which have the effect of stimulating their own insulin production. But many diabetics cannot survive without daily injections of insulin. For them, the final result of a lack of insulin is likely to be diabetic coma and subsequent death. The inmate cannot go elsewhere for assistance —she must depend on you, the prison personnel. On the other hand, insulin reaction, less serious and always possible even in the best-controlled diabetics, may be more easily prevented in the limited correctional environment. Diabetic inmates, once placed on a proper regimen, usually require no other special treatment.

A knowledge of the symptoms of undetected diabetics may be helpful. Some of them are excessive thirst, excessive urination, hunger, loss of weight, easy tiring, slow healing of cuts and bruises, changes in vision, intense itching, pain in fingers and toes, and drowsiness.

Compare the symptoms of insulin reaction with those of diabetic coma:

Characteristic	Insulin Reaction	Diabetic Coma
Onset	Sudden	Gradual
Skin	Pale (may be moist)	Flushed, dry
Behavior	Disoriented (or confused)	Drowsy
Breath	Normal	Fruity odor (acetone)
Breathing	Normal to rapid, shallow	Deep, labored
Vomiting	Absent	Present
Tongue	Moist	Dry
Hunger	Present	Absent
Thirst	Absent	Present
Sugar in urine	Absent or slight	Large amounts

A wide range of informational materials on diabetes can be obtained from the American Diabetes Association, Inc., 18 East 48th Street, New York, New York, 10017.

Many publications are available without charge, others at only a nominal cost. Diet lists can be obtained upon request, as can information concerning diabetes-detection programs.

An understanding of diabetes will help correctional personnel to care for diabetic inmates, although no correctional personnel should or can be expected to serve as a physician.

With proper attention, the otherwise healthy diabetic inmate can live and work in the same way as the nondiabetic.

Epilepsy

It is now possible to increase the rehabilitative opportunities offered to epileptic inmates in a correctional setting. It is estimated that the incidence of epilepsy in the general population is 1 in each 200 persons. As a result of a partial survey made by the New York State Department of Correction as of December 31, 1955, 1 in every 126 inmates had the diagnostic label "epileptic."[4]

It has been estimated that 50 percent of epileptics can have their seizures completely controlled, and an additional 30 percent can have their seizures reduced in frequency or severity to an extent that they can become self-supporting. The main pharmacological device to effect the control of seizures is the anticonvulsant. While the total therapeutic front must include purposeful activity in addition to a more enlightened and accepting approach to the physical handicap of epilepsy, the main

---

[4] Dansereau, Raymond A.: Epilepsy and anticonvulsants in a correctional setting. *American Journal of Correction*, March-April, 1964, p. 22.

weapon is the anticonvulsant which either alters the metabolism or chemistry of the neurons which give rise to the unregulated discharge of electric current which results in a seizure. Although there are other therapeutic devices supplementary to the anticonvulsants, there is no real substitute for them.

With control of seizures and a continued medical regimen, epileptics may safely engage in activities from which they have been traditionally excluded, such as work around moving machinery, and various athletic activities.

As part of a staff training program, the following suggested procedures for handling an inmate in a seizure should be mimeographed and distributed.

IMMEDIATE ASSISTANCE WHEN A PERSON HAS A GRAND MAL SEIZURE[5]

1. Keep calm, as any level-headed individual can handle the situation. The epileptic seizure in itself is not dangerous. However, injuries may result from the fall or unconsciousness.
2. If noticed in time, the person should be lowered to the floor. If her mouth is not yet closed tightly, a padded tongue depressor or rolled handkerchief may be inserted between her back teeth to prevent tongue and cheek biting. Do not try to open mouth.
3. Restrictive clothing at her neck should be loosened to make the person more comfortable.
4. Remove from the area any furniture or other items she may strike during the clonic stage of her convulsion.
5. A pillow, folded shirt, or substitute placed under her head will help to prevent injury on a hard floor. When the person falls to or is helped to the floor, the tonic phase already has started and will be seen as a rigidity or stiffness of the body muscles. After a few seconds, the seizure passes into the clonic phase. Rigidity is replaced by jerking movements involving the whole body. During the seizure, the lips and face may turn bluish, a cry or throat noise as air is exhaled may be heard, excessive saliva flow (foaming) may occur, loss of bladder or bowel control may also occur. The seizure is followed by fatigue, possibly a state of half awareness, or deep sleep.
6. It is necessary that the patient be allowed to rest in order for full recovery to take place. The speed of recovery and amount of time for it varies from person to person.

---

[5] *Ibid.*, p. 23.

7. Do not leave the patient recovering from a seizure unattended as she may be in a confused state or may bury her face in a pillow and have trouble breathing.

MEDICAL ASSISTANCE IS REQUIRED IN CERTAIN SPECIFIC CASES

1. A physical injury is suffered as a result of seizure.
2. Seizures follow one another so closely that the patient does not regain consciousness. If rigidity is followed by jerking movements, then again rigidity and jerking movements, etc., a condition known as status epilepticus prevails.

As with any physical handicap which sets an individual apart from his fellowman or requires a medical regimen, the groundwork is laid for an adjustment pattern which is different from that found in so-called "normal" people. Two such reactions that may very well occur in an epileptic associated with her physical handicap are first, a feeling of inferiority or a feeling of decreased personal worth which one frequently gets as a result of being a "pill-taker." Frequently the person with epilepsy does not want to admit to herself that she has epilepsy and also wants to conceal this fact from persons around her. Second, the individual may believe because she is taking anticonvulsants, she must receive or demand that preferential treatment because of her handicap. When either of the above feelings present themselves, they require the approach of counseling.

A feeling of inferiority or a feeling of decreased personal worth is a counseling problem. An inmate's attempt to get preferential treatment because she has to take anticonvulsants must take a twofold approach: one, counseling and two, a regime requiring certain types of performances which indicate to the inmate that, with rare exceptions, the standards that apply to inmates generally in the institution also apply to her.

It is possible for an inmate to equate taking medication with punishment. This can come about because the inmate is required in a correctional setting to carry out certain routines which are necessary for a well-ordered institution. From the viewpoint of the institution, an inmate must take her anticonvulsant if it is prescribed for her. Taking anticonvulsants may then become

one of the onerous routines which exist in a correctional setting.
If a correction officer administers the medication, this increases
the likelihood of the inmate equating taking the medication with
punishment. This requires in part a counseling approach and
in part a change in routines connected with the administration
of medication. In counseling, the inmate should be made to
understand and accept the notion that the medication is for her
own benefit rather than something that is imposed upon her.
The routines can be changed by placing the responsibility with
medical personnel rather than custodial personnel for the administration of anticonvulsants.

It is possible that an inmate will become so dependent upon
medication that she will be reluctant to cease taking it or have
the amount reduced when it is so prescribed by a physician. This
comes about because a more intelligent person can see the
relationship between a consumption of medication and a reduction
or absence of seizures. Because of the anxiety connected with
the possibility of having a seizure or the embarrassment of
having a seizure, a given individual may believe that she would
be better off taking the medication at a given level and not
attempt either to taper it off or eventually give it up if recommended by the physician. This, too, is primarily a counseling
problem. What to strive for here is a knowledge on the part of
the inmate as to what anticonvulsants do, as well as her developing a feeling of confidence in the institution physician and the
physician which she is free to choose on the outside so that she
will follow whatever suggestions and prescriptions he will
give her.

Drug Addicts

Drug addiction among women is steadily increasing, and
its treatment up to now has been virtually ineffectual and unrealistic.[6] In women's prisons, this problem will be most prevalent in those states having large urban populations, such as
California, Illinois, and the Northeastern states. Those states

---

[6] Brummit, Houston: Observations on drug addicts in a house of detention
for women. *Corrective Psychiatry and Journal of Social Therapy,* Second Quarter,
1963, p. 62.

primarily rural, such as the southern and midwestern states, will have comparatively few addicts.

The first phase in the treatment program for addicts is the withdrawal of narcotics. Methadone is substituted for the various narcotics used by inmates and reduced gradually but rapidly in amount.[7] If an inmate is also addicted to barbiturates, a similar but slower gradual reduction is carried on simultaneously. The average time for withdrawal is about a week, but may range from a day or two to three or four weeks. The withdrawal procedure varies from individual to individual, the time required depending on many factors, most important of these being the drug used, the quantity used, and the physical condition of the inmate. Inmates have usually been withdrawn from drugs before they arrive at the prison. However, many counties have no facilities for withdrawal other than "cold turkey." Because of the screaming and noise associated with this type of withdrawal, some inmates are kept on drugs until they are delivered to the prison. Parole violators are often brought straight to the prison, with no time for withdrawal before arriving.

During the withdrawal phase, the inmate is physically ill and uncomfortable. The inmate can be assured that she will be withdrawn slowly enough so that there will be no danger and so that the discomfort is minimized. However, she should also know that the medical staff will withdraw her as rapidly as possible and that she is bound to suffer some discomfort.

Aside from heroin addiction, the greatest common factor among drug addicts is the rejecting home environment. Although many addicts are products of broken homes, the majority share a history of brutal parents. Dynamically there has been marked conflict centered on one parent from whom the addict never gained approval. In the addict's endless search for this acceptance, she has generally acted out her hostility against less important "approval" objects, namely school teachers, truant officers, and authority in general. For the most part, they have been placed at a young age in our various corrective institutions where they have learned from other inmates more wonders of

---

[7] O'Donnell, John A.: The Lexington program for narcotic addicts. *Federal Probation*, March, 1962, p. 56.

drug addiction and other antisocial vices. Outside of the institutions, an underworld society is formed and its members freely engage in prostitution, homosexuality, various degrees of larceny, illegal gambling, marijuana smoking, and occasional alcoholism. This society, in which the search for love never ends and pleasure becomes paramount, is known as " the life."[8] Since the parents have been the original disapprovers, the search will continue in a usually futile effort to find a satisfactory compromise.

Intense hatred or anger represents the primary emotion or feeling all inmates have in common with one another. Some show it overtly and verbalize these feelings toward staff and fellow prisoners. Others are hostile in their behavior and act and dress like callous teen-age male delinquents. The majority are unaware of their hostility and instead tend to cooperate, participate actively in prison routines, and seek to better themselves. The latter also have headaches, speak of tension, have stomach disorders, and frequent the medical clinics.

The psychiatric constituency of the prison population is very much akin to that seen in mental hospitals except that there are fewer schizophrenics and more passive-aggressive personalities.[9]

One approach in therapy that should be seriously considered in women's prisons is that used in the House of Detention for Women, New York City.[10] Where attempts have been made to conduct psychotherapy, they have tried to drain the anger of the inmates. The first step has been to capture their imagination or introspective curiosity and work toward their seeing themselves in perspective. This is a very difficult task, since most of the women in prison represent a hard-core, embittered slum or middle-class group, mistrustful of society. Very often, when these people have been reared in a milieu of self-contempt, they think in terms of hate and are without a specific object for this hate and attendant antisocial behavior.

In group sessions, they have sought to get the inmates to directly explore their repressed and suppressed feelings and

---

[8] Brummit, *op. cit.* p. 64.

[9] *Ibid.* p. 62.

[10] *Ibid.* pp. 62-70.

experiences centered on hate. Since, almost without exception, in their brief anamneses they describe hypercritical or sadistic parents, the staff simply encourages them to talk about which-ever parent was the worse. This frank approach is surprising to the inmate but very productive. In the beginning, it may be difficult for them to bring up the ugly thoughts, for in our society we are taught to "honor thy father and mother." Very often the inmates recant fantastic childhood tales of incest, murder, and flabbergasting hypocrisy. The thought that they might resent their parents for the injustices they have committed remains dormant and displaced at first.

Since in our society aggression and the expression of anger are not condoned, the angry inmate vents her hostility toward the wrong authority figures. In the past it was the parents who established the original model. The inmates therefore need greater understanding of themselves and their emotional conflicts so as to learn exactly who is the "enemy." Once they are able to see themselves more objectively and gain insight into their personalities, they may have less need to be self-destructive and antisocial. By distinguishing between their parents and society, they might be able to accept the rules and regulations of society with which, in the past, they have come into conflict.

Thus the orientation of therapy must necessarily take a dynamic, more practical slant, geared toward the experiences and needs of the inmates. The emphasis should therefore be reconstructive and educational. Having lived in a fringed, unsocial society during their formative years, they are usually overly sophisticated in certain spheres and amazingly naive in others. (In this sexually polymorphous group, sexuality is not one of their paramount problems.) The focus should be on how to integrate and survive in society. Having lived in institutions and the underworld for so many years, their ability to adjust in a normal community has hibernated in a fog of addiction and confinement. The inmate who seeks to change her status wants to know how to go about getting self-discipline, what other social outlets are available, what kind of work she can get, what opportunities are open to her, and where she can live. Inmates are shy and frightened in considering what they intend to do on the outside, what plans are realistic or unwise, and what they would like to make of themselves. It is the purpose of such influence to motivate the women toward those positive forces that promote their recovery.

In many instances, a total rehabilitative program is indicated, as many inmates are long-term products of our institutions and have attended the graduated series of treatment-oriented institutions, training school, and state prisons. They know of no other existence than that of "the life" and the structure of an institution; for them, psychotherapy or counseling should be more instructive and reeducational rather than analytic.

Clinical impressions[11] suggest the relapse to drug use may well vary geographically, with higher rates of relapse in the metropolitan centers like New York and Chicago where the number of addicts is higher. Studies[12] indicate that supervision, and particularly intensive supervision, produces lower relapse rates, at least for the periods of supervision.

Clinical impressions[13] (still not corroborated by research) also suggest that for at least some patients, success in abstaining from drugs is associated with a move away from the area in which the person was addicted. If this turns out to be correct, it will probably be explainable not as a simple function of availability of drugs but rather as removal of the person from all of the cues and reminders of previous drug use.

We should bear in mind that the community suffers along with the inmate, for the addict habit is supported through illegal activities and often brutal assault upon the citizens of the community. It is reasonable to assume that there is a strong positive correlation between drug addiction and the crime rate.

The Aged Inmate

One problem common to all women's prisons is the wide range in ages of the inmates—from teen-age girls to senile women. An understanding of the aging process should help prison personnel to be better prepared to meet this problem.

---

[11] O'Donnell, *op. cit.* p. 59.
[12] *Ibid.*
[13] *Ibid.*

As age advances, individuals develop arteriosclerosis and senility. However, the amount of arteriosclerosis and/or senility in any one individual varies extremely in relation to the age. In other words, some people become old while young, and some people remain young while old.

People who develop arteriosclerosis are subject to, and indeed frequently become afflicted with, chronic debilitating diseases such as those of the kidneys and heart. Or, as a result of sclerosis of the arteries of the brain, such people are subject to strokes. Also, as a result of arteriosclerosis of the peripheral arteries, people are subject to high blood pressure and peripheral vascular disease. Of course, all these conditions result in disability to a lesser or greater degree, depending upon the type, duration, and extent of the disease developed as a result of the arterial changes. It is to be realized, then, that any inmate who looks or seems old may be suffering from any one of the diseases or any combination (and usually it is a combination) of the diseases mentioned above. These individuals may have an accumulation of waste products in their system which adversely affects their health in general. They may have shortness of breath. They may have pain in the chest. They may have poor nourishment to the brain, which interferes with memory and other mental functions. They may have headaches from high blood pressure. And they are subject to an attack of heart failure or stroke, or terminal kidney failure, spoken of as uremia. Because of their physical condition, therefore, it is obvious that such inmates require considerably different treatment from those inmates who are younger and free of senility and arteriosclerosis.

The diet of older people should not contain an excess of protein and should contain very little fat, unless, of course, they are undernourished and underweight. A high-carbohydrate diet is excellent for elderly people. Foods containing cholesterol may hasten arteriosclerosis and therefore shorten life. Foods high in cholesterol are egg yolks, butter, the fat part of milk, and animal fats. Elderly people should masticate their foods thoroughly to facilitate digestion, and overeating is strictly to be avoided.[14]

---

[14] Baier, George F., III: The aged inmate. *American Journal of Correction*, March-April, 1961, p. 4.

In old people, so-called indigestion is quite commonly due to heart disease rather than to intestinal, gall bladder, or stomach trouble. An attack of acute indigestion in an elderly person quite often turns out to be a heart attack, called coronary thrombosis. Also pain in the calves precipitated by walking is a symptom of arteriosclerosis and is therefore not uncommon in elderly people. Dizziness and headache also are common symptoms of aging arteries.

It has often been said that individuals are as old as their arteries. This is quite true. Old age, however, does not necessarily imply chronic illness; yet most of the disabilities that come about in old age and the misery that they bring and the uselessness that results are consequences of chronic degenerative diseases and not of age per se.

In addition to the physical change, inmates who are arteriosclerotic and senile undergo characteristic mental and personality changes. In older people, there is a greater difference between individuals; two old people are much more unlike than two young people. This is true because people change as a result of their experiences, and older people have had more experiences. They have had more injuries, more physical insults, more diseases, more emotional trauma, more social encounters, more successes, more failures. Hence, successful dealing with older people absolutely necessitates individualization.

Another important point in dealing with older inmates is recognizing that their tolerance for stress and strain of all types is diminished. Their ability to maintain equilibrium is slow and imperfect. In other words, older people cannot adjust as well as younger people to anything—to changes of temperature, changes in food, changes of habit, changes in living quarters, or changes of environment. Minor things can readily disturb their balance of both physical and mental health.

Symptoms and signs of disease in the aged are much less conspicuous than in younger people. In a similar disease of a similar extent and severity, an older person will have less fever, less pain, less rapid pulse, less swelling, less diarrhea, etc. So, manifestations of various diseases are much less easily recognized. Appendicitis can be readily overlooked, and the same is particularly true for intestinal obstruction, septicemia, pneumonia, diabetes, and tuberculosis. By the same token, minor deviations and subtle suggestions of dysfunction take on a much greater significance. And, therefore, severity of symptoms is wholly unreliable in evaluating the severity of disease in the elderly.

Correctional officers, as well as the medical staff, should realize also that repair and healing in the aged are very slow. Wound healing is retarded. A much longer time is required to recover from an infection. Convalescence must be prolonged, and patience on the part of all concerned is therefore necessary. Exercise, for example, can be increased only very slightly each day in the process of rehabilitating an elderly person who has been immobilized temporarily as a result of disease or injury. Just a trifle more each day can be tolerated; yet this trifle more must be insisted upon in order to progress with the rehabilitation of such individuals who have, of necessity, been at bed rest.

It should also be mentioned that elderly people require and must be given much smaller dosages of drugs. The drugs are absorbed more slowly, though sometimes less completely. Their elimination is also diminished, and because of this, drugs are likely to accumulate in the system, especially if there is circulatory impairment or kidney dysfunction, both of which are common in the elderly. Sedative drugs, particularly barbiturates, are poorly tolerated by the elderly; they produce disorientation, forgetfulness, apprehension, and unsteadiness.

It probably does not need to be mentioned that memory, especially for recent events, becomes very unreliable with age. There is loss of acuity of the special senses that assist in memory. And if the will to remember is less, so is the motivation to remember. Details become much less significant, impressions become less brilliant, and attention becomes less intent. Regardless of the factors that result in poor memory, the correctional officers and medical staff members must remember that elderly inmates cannot be expected to remember what they are told. Patience, thoroughness, simplicity, and repetition are essential in instructing or assisting the elderly inmate. All instructions must be precisely specific, and if they are at all important, they must be written out clearly and unmistakably.

It might also be mentioned that the truly aged frequently feel extremely insecure. Prison frightens them, illness frightens them, new faces frighten them, correctional officers frighten them, authority frightens them, other inmates frighten them, financial insecurity frightens them, the future frightens them, the realization of their loss of strength and vigor frightens them, the fear of death in prison frightens them. Every opportunity should be taken to improve their morale and to give them encouragement. Effort should be made to improve their family relations, as this is a very important element affecting their emotional tranquility. Aggressive incorrigibles should not be housed with them, for probably nothing can be more panic provoking to an aged or infirm inmate.

Elderly inmates are extremely grateful for assistance, kindness, and patience. They are as helpless as children but not unappreciative like children. On the other hand, do not do too much for them, for it is important that they continue to maintain a maximum degree of self-sufficiency.

The supreme tragedy of senility is the awareness of uselessness. Aged persons may realize that they are not needed by their family, society, or by anyone. They feel the rejection. A purposeless existence predisposes them to psychological imbalance and mental breakdown. Elderly inmates must be given hope, and one of the greatest hopes they can be given is a hope that they will have something purposeful to do in life, a place in life. In order to accomplish this, they must be given a job, a place, a thing to do in prison. If this is not accomplished, elderly inmates are likely to feel that people who are closest to them no longer want them and are merely waiting for them to die. When such an attitude or idea is engendered in their minds, it can rightfully be expected that paranoid antagonism will be created and may indeed be acted upon violently.

There is a greater hazard for the aged in being too restricted in their activities than there is in their overdoing. Consequently, elderly people must be allowed to continue their occupation, even if it may mean the danger of a tragedy occurring as a result of physical disease. In other words, at all costs, their life should be made as happy and contended as possible. The correctional officers should encourage physical and mental activities and general interests, realizing that the patient is more important than her illness.

Inmates in wheel chairs present a special problem. An attendant, another inmate, can be assigned on a volunteer basis to such an inmate to help her in and out of her wheelchair, in and out of bed, etc. She will often also need help to get to and from the commode and to assist in this and to help her support herself while on the commode, rails made of one-inch plumbing pipe can be placed on each side of a commode.

Idleness and unemployment in this age group are naturally difficult to avoid but can be prevented through concerted efforts of a coordinated institutional staff. Part-time work should be undertaken in every possible case.

Programs in themselves are not as important a factor in their success as is the attitude of the individuals who conduct them. Success in treating patients must start with establishing rapport. This requires, first and foremost, that inmates be confronted with an attitude and atmosphere of sympathetic understanding. Following this, there must be politeness, and finally, there must be a genuine show of interest in the disabled inmate.

Rejection is incompatible with treatment. The attitude towards disabled inmates opens or obstructs the inmates' road to higher virtues. Inmates don't act, they react. If we have them realize that we believe they are good, kind, just, and fair, they will be at their best.

Physically incapacitated inmates are likely to feel inadequate. And it is well to recognize that inadequacies are often the hidden force behind aggressive behavior. In such cases, it is important that correctional officers control their temper.

Probably one of the most distressing features in dealing with disabled and debilitated inmates is the uncertainty which pertains to the results the staff, as individuals, will obtain. In absolute truth, the aim is the unattainable, and correctional workers must be content with finding few successes and many failures in striving toward complete rehabilitation.

Patience and cheerfulness will be the best tools, and if we will combine persistency with these, we will have at least a memory of a well-spent life in helping others who depend upon us.

The Dental Program

A vital part of the initial physical examination of newly arrived inmates is a thorough dental examination. After examination of the inmate, a record should be made on an appropriate card giving the date, diagnosis, and any treatment required. The normal and abnormal conditions of the mouth should be noted. If the inmate is in pain, immediate treatment should be given and the patient told to return for subsequent treatment. At this time, x-rays, extractions, fillings, and minor oral surgery may be performed when necessary. Other treatment includes the oral administration of antibiotics, prophylaxis (cleaning), and the treatment of lacerations and lesions of the lip.

In addition to individual records, daily and monthly records of dental work performed should also be maintained.

In women inmates, a high incidence of broken, infected, and carious teeth are the result of beatings, drug addiction, or lack of care. Many of these women have never owned a toothbrush, do not care to, or cannot afford one. Instruction in dental hygiene has been preponderantly lacking from their education. Part of the dentist's duty, therefore, should be to give talks to the inmates on the proper care of teeth and mouth. The importance of correct brushing can be demontrated with a model toothbrush. If an inmate cannot afford a toothbrush and toothpaste, she should be able to secure them through the medical department.

Movies on the subject of oral hygiene can be shown with great advantage to the inmate. When films are scheduled anyway, a short trailer can be shown for educational purposes along with the usual picture for entertainment.

Another routine duty of the dentist is making a special effort to detect any indication of a systemic disease, such as leukemia, anemia, syphilis, measles, and Vincent's infection. Should there be evidence of such a disease, the inmate should be isolated and medical consultation and treatment requested.

Conditions such as fractured jaws, Ludwig's angina (infectious disease), and marked swelling should be given emergency treatment. Impaction may be removed, but these cases are better off when sent to the hospital rather than treated in the clinic. In the hospital, the inmate can be given the proper bed rest and the required postoperative treatment.

Restorative treatment such as the repairing or replacing of missing crowns and teeth, bridges, or full dentures, are deferred for attention at a later date.

Like any patient, the inmate is often afraid of the dentist. But unlike other patients, she must submit to a routine examination as part of her medical record. After this, she can reserve the right to refuse, though every inmate may apply for treatment in an emergency.

Most women's prisons are too small to require the services of a full-time dentist. However, the part-time dentist should have the services of an oral hygienist to assist him. The hygienist can institute prophylactic treatment and can assist with the preparation and during minor surgery. Other duties would include taking x-rays and developing them, sterilizing instruments, and setting up an instrument tray for the next patient. If the prison cannot afford an oral hygienist and must use an inmate as a dental-chair assistant, an officer should be present at all times.

Certain phases of dentistry offer an excellent vocational training program. One of these is a prosthetic laboratory to train dental laboratory technicians to learn the mechanical dentistry that is indispensable to prosthetics. Inmates may be taught the methods for repairing and making artificial restorations from impressions taken by the dentist in a schedule of schooling that would require approximately two to three years of time. The learning of this particular trade would serve at least two important functions. First, there is a great demand for dental laboratory technicians in private practice. The inmate, when released into normal life, would then have a substantial head start toward earning an ample legitimate living. Secondly, with regard to the institution arrangement itself, the mechanical dental work could then be done by the inmates themselves, right on the premises. This would be a boon to the budget.

A typical prosthetic laboratory to handle the needs of approximately five hundred inmates would include the following: several benches and equipment to accommodate about five technicians in a room of about 25 feet by 30 feet. These averages are based on the observation that usually one-third of the inmates require partial dentures and 2 to 5 per cent of the inmates need full restorations.[15]

The dentist is an important liaison between correctional officer and inmate. Proper dental care may induce the inmate to develop good habits of personal cleanliness and neat appearance. When she is relieved of pain in the mouth, such a patient is often less likely to be arrogant, belligerent, hostile, and disorderly, for she realizes that someone does care and is interested in her welfare. Thus the practice of dentistry within the correctional institution plays a vital role in our society's control of crime.

Eye Examinations

As vital as the dental examination is an eye examination, including a test for glaucoma, as a part of the initial physical examination. Each inmate needing glasses should be furnished them at the earliest date.

When finances are insufficient to meet such needs as eyeglasses and the inmate is unable to pay for them herself, the aid of fraternal organizations (such as the Lion's Club, whose goal is sight preservation) may be enlisted.

Outpatient Department

The outpatient department functions as the center of the health and medical services. There should be a regular clinic call presided over by the physician at a designated hour, preferably at a time that interferes least with the total program. The clinic nurse should screen requests to see the doctor and treat women with minor ailments. Except in emergencies, all requests for medication or treatment should be seen during regular clinic hours.

---

[15] Singer, Philip L.: Dental care programs in correctional institutions. *American Journal of Correction,* Jan.-Feb., 1966, p. 10.

It will be necessary to run a "pill line" two or three times a day for those women on prescribed medications. At this time P.R.M.s for headaches and cramps can be dispensed, as well as laxatives. Care must be taken to insure that women swallow medications.

VOCATIONAL REHABILITATION

The Vocational Rehabilitation Administration made medical services available to the disabled in 1943. At this time, it also altered the definition of disability to include mental handicaps. The most recent legislative improvements took place in November 1965, with the passage of Public Law 89-333, the "Amendments to the Vocational Rehabilitation Act." These amendments enlarge the opportunities for VRA contributions to the correctional field.

Teaching grants and innovation and expansion grant programs, created by the 1965 amendments to develop new projects in correctional rehabilitation will be discussed in another chapter of this book. This discussion will center on the medical aspects of the Vocational Rehabilitation Administration.

Many public offenders are, in fact, disabled persons and are therefore eligible for as many of these programs and services as may be required. The actual services are performed or arranged for by professional rehabilitation counselors working within the state rehabilitation agencies.

The counselor generally begins his service with a complete evaluation of his client. He arranges for a medical examination and for psychological or psychiatric studies. Work-evaluation procedures are used to determine the client's vocational interests and aptitudes. After defining the extent of the client's problem, the counselor works with her to plan the necessary rehabilitation services. Depending on the needs of the individual case, these may include:

1. Physical restoration which provides medical treatment to alleviate conditions preventing employment, artificial limbs and appliances, and hospitalization if required. Cosmetic surgery may be performed on individuals whose disfigurement may be a negative factor in their attempts to adjust to society. Provision may also be made for short-term psychiatric treatment or psychotherapy.

2. Vocational training which helps to qualify the disabled person for employment in occupations within her physical and mental capacities. This can refer to instruction of almost any kind, ranging from on-the-job training to a college education.

3. Vocational counseling which assists the rehabilitated client in selecting a realistic job goal—one that reflects her interests and aptitudes.

4. Job placement, the final phase of the process which seeks to secure appropriate employment for the rehabilitated client. This may be in the competitive job market, in a sheltered workshop, or in a homebound environment. Regardless of the type of placement, the counselor follows up his employed client to make sure that she is satisfied and that her employer is satisfied with her. Services to promote employment of the handicapped may include provision of occupational tools and equipment, licenses, and help in starting small business enterprises.

The counselor may also work closely with the client's immediate family, providing special services designed to establish a home atmosphere conducive to the client's rehabilitation and to her continuing success in her new job.

With the new vocational rehabilitation amendments, there is scarcely a limit to the advantages which correctional agencies may now fit into their programs.

Medical Training Programs

The medical program should include a training program not only for staff but also for inmates. The medical field contains some of the most urgently needed vocational training programs.

If the prison is large enough, nurses aides and laboratory technical aides can be trained in the prison hospital. Training for licensed practical nurses is much more complicated than can be completed in most women's prisons. However, such a program is possible in conjunction with an outside affiliation. Classroom requirements can be met within the prison, and practical experience can be gained through a state mental hospital, county hospital, or other nearby hospital. These inmates must be chosen with extreme care, and the program must meet the standards of the State Department of Education, in order that the inmates may be licensed upon completion of the program.

The small Minnesota Prison for Women has had a very successful program in working with mentally retarded girls. This is a joint endeavor with the state Mental Health Department and is financed through the Mental Health Department. A cottage for mentally retarded girls under the age of twelve has been constructed within the prison grounds. Although it is staffed by mental health professional personnel, inmates work closely with the staff in the care of the girls. This program is mutually beneficial to both the institutions and the inmates; the institutions financially and the inmates through the educational program and though the exchange of T.L.C. between the girls and inmates. The program is under the supervision of the superintendent of the women's prison.

A training program in the dental department has been described in the section pertaining to dental services.

ADDITIONAL RESPONSIBILITIES OF THE MEDICAL SERVICES

In the preventive health area, the medical service should provide inspection and advice on matters relating to institution sanitation, including food handling and preparation, and milk and water supply.

A member of the medical department is represented on the safety committee. This committee is to insure a comprehensive safety program at the institution, to insure the proper reporting of all accidents, and to improve safety and sanitation procedures and standards.

A member of the medical staff should make rounds daily to check on the health of each woman in Locked status.

In the event of an inmate's death, the medical department has the responsibility of seeing that all necessary procedures, county and statewide, are adhered to.

It is the responsibility of the medical department to make recommendations for the transfer of an inmate to a mental hospital and to effect the transfer of the patient from the institution to the mental hospital.

SUMMARY

Upon entering prison, an inmate's self is systematically, if often unintentionally, mortified. Care must be taken that during the physical examination unnecessary degradations do not occur. As in every other phase of the operation of a women's prison, human dignity must be respected.

The physician or nurse administratively in charge of the medical services of an institution is directly responsible to the superintendent of the institution.

It would be well for institutions having only part-time services of a physician to consider using a resident in obstetrics and gynecology from a nearby hospital as the institution physician. Those institutions unable to afford medical personnel might hire L.P.N.'s as matrons, thereby insuring some degree of medical knowledge on the staff.

By using the facilities of nearby hospitals and men's institutions, women's institutions can avoid the need for elaborate and expensive medical quarters and equipment. Selected inmates may be sent to the hospital without guards. Temporary paroles may be granted to inmates during their stay in the hospital. In cases necessitating guards, private nurses may be used when the custodial staff is too small to be able to cover this extra post.

The physical examination of each newly arrived inmate should include chest x-rays, Pap smear, dental and eye examinations. Necessary medical, dental, and eye conditions should be treated as diagnosed, and each new arrival should receive indicated immunizations.

Pregnant inmates and babies born to inmates pose a particular problem for all women's institutions. Flexibility should allow for the mother who has only a short period of her sentence left and who is in a position to care for her baby when she returns to the community to care for her baby in the institution until she leaves.

Correctional administrators and workers should become familiar with the behavior of diabetics who are experiencing insulin reaction or its direct opposite, diabetic coma. Every diabetic who takes insulin should have some form of sugar available at all times.

The incidence of epilepsy is almost twice as great in prison as it is in the general population. As part of a staff training program, there are suggested procedures for handling an inmate in a seizure. These could be mimeographed and distributed to the staff.

Drug addiction among women is steadily increasing. An approach to therapy which has been used in the House of Detention for Women in New York City has been to get the inmates to directly explore their repressed and suppressed feelings and experiences centered on hate. The inmates need greater understanding of themselves and their emotional conflicts so as to learn exactly whom to hate. For these inmates, psychotherapy or counseling should be more instructive and reeducational rather than analytic.

Because they must accept offenders ranging in age from teen-age girls to senile women, all institutions for women have difficult problems. It is to be realized that any inmate who looks or seems old may be suffering from any one of the diseases or combination of diseases associated with aging. Because of their physical condition, therefore, it is obvious that such inmates require considerably different treatment from those inmates who are younger and free of senility and arteriosclerosis. The diet of older people should not contain an excess of protein, but a high-carbohydrate diet is excellent for them. Another important point in dealing with older inmates is recognizing that their tolerance for stress and strain of all types is diminished. Symptoms and signs of disease in the aged are much less conspicuous than in younger people. Also, repair and healing in the aged are very slow. Elderly people require and must be given much smaller dosages of drugs. Memory becomes very unreliable with age. All instructions must be precisely specific, and if they are at all important, they must be written out clearly and unmistakably. Truly aged people frequently feel extremely insecure. Elderly inmates must be given hope, and one of the greatest hopes they can be given is a hope that they will have something purposeful to do in life. Officers should encourage physical and mental activities and general interests, realizing that the inmate is more important than her illness.

With the new vocational rehabilitation amendments, there is scarcely a limit to the advantages which correctional agencies may now fit into their programs, for many public offenders are, in fact, disabled persons and are therefore eligible for as many of these programs and services as may be required.

A member of the medical staff should make rounds daily to check on the health of each woman in Locked status.

There should be a regular outpatient clinic presided over by a doctor. Requests to see the doctor should be screened by the clinic nurse. Medication is dispensed several times daily at the "pill line." The medical department spends considerable time and effort in diagnosing, treating, and prescribing medication in order to maintain a high level of physical fitness among the inmate population. Obviously, if the treatment ordered or the medication prescribed is not taken, no benefit can be obtained. Matrons often have the responsibility to insure that the medication is not only available to the inmate but is administered as directed by the medical department. In order that maximum benefit be obtained, the medical department must receive accurate reports from these matrons as to the disposition of the medication.

BIBLIOGRAPHY

Books

American Correctional Association: *Manual of Correctional Standards.* New York, the American Correctional Association, 1966.
Goffman, Erving: *Asylums.* Garden City, Doubleday, 1961.

Periodicals

Babcock, Lyndon: Hypnotherapy in the prison setting. *American Journal of Correction,* May-June, 1967, pp. 10-12.
Baier, George F.: The aged inmate. *American Journal of Correction,* March-April, 1961, pp. 4-6, 30, 34.
Berliner, Arthur K.: The helping process in a hospital for narcotic addicts. *Federal Probation,* September, 1962, pp. 57-62.
Bummit, Houston: Observations on drug addicts in a house of detention for

women. *Corrective Psychiatry and Journal of Social Therapy,* Second Quarter, 1963, pp. 62-70.

Casper, Elizabeth W.: Crime and mental illness. *Corrective Psychiatry and Journal of Social Therapy,* March, 1965, pp. 73-84.

Clanon, T. L.: Persecutory feeling and self-mutilation in prisoners. *Corrective Psychiatry and Journal of Social Therapy,* March, 1965, pp. 96-102.

Dansereau, Raymond A.: Epilepsy and anticonvulsants in a correctional setting. *American Journal of Correction,* March-April, 1964, pp. 22-25.

Finlayson, Malcolm: The functions of a psychiatrist in a prison. *Corrective Psychiatry and Journal of Social Therapy,* Third Quarter, 1961, pp. 135-143.

Heller, Melvin S., and Sadoff, Robert L.: Experiences with a university-affiliated psychiatric service in a correctional institution. *Corrective Psychiatry and Journal of Social Therapy,* May, 1966, pp. 258-262.

Leland, Tom W.: Part-time psychiatric consultation in a prison. *Corrective Psychiatry and Journal of Social Therapy,* July, 1965, pp. 196-203.

Newberg, Paula M.: A study of how the concept of self is affected by incarceration. *Corrective Psychiatry and Journal of Social Therapy,* May, 1966, pp. 258-262.

O'Donnell, John A.: The Lexington program for narcotic addicts. *Federal Probation,* March, 1962, pp. 55-60.

Peck, Franklin B.: Some facts about diabetic inmates of correctional institutions. *American Journal of Correction,* March-April, 1962, pp. 22-23.

Peterson, David M., Yarvis, Richard M., and Farkas, Gerald M.: The Federal Bureau of Prisons treatment program for narcotic addicts. *Federal Probation,* June, 1969, pp. 35-40.

Singer, Philip L.: Dental care programs in correctional institutions. *American Journal of Correction,* January-February, 1966, pp. 8-10, 12.

Switzer, Mary E.: Vocational rehabilitation and corrections: a promising partnership. *Federal Probation,* September, 1967, pp. 12-17.

Chapter 5

BUILDINGS AND GROUNDS

THE BUILDINGS AND GROUNDS of a women's prison should reflect the program of the institution. If a new prison is to be built, the first step in development is to study the program or proposed program and then to design the institution to meet these needs.

Housing should serve classification purposes, not only by providing varying degrees of custody but also by creating different types of situations in which to test apparent improvement in inmate attitudes. For this reason, an institution for women should be equipped with several types of housing— single rooms if at all possible; if not, perhaps small wards and very definitely maximum security cells.

An institution for women should be located in an uncongested area within easy traveling distance by bus or automobile of a community large enough to provide cultural opportunities for staff, educational opportunities for the children of the staff, and one large enough to provide the community contacts which are essential for a good program.

All facilities should be constructed with the possibility of future expansion.

The rehabilitation program for women requires living in small groups in as natural a situation as can be achieved under the circumstances, with provision for homemaking opportunities. Small kitchenettes should be provided.

Generally, the open-court overall arrangement of buildings has been found satisfactory, with the administration, hospital, school, and security area at one end and the industrial and recreational areas at the far end. Care must be taken not to spread too wide apart the areas that require 24-hour custody control.

One-story structures generally are preferred. They reduce the supervisory personnel required, eliminate hidden areas, and simplify maintenance.

Cottages of about forty capacity, divided into two units, twenty each, with their own lounges or day rooms and kitchenettes have been found satisfactory. Single rooms are essential.

Cottages should be well-spaced so as to permit the less active recreation in the immediate vicinity of the cottage within the open court. This and the placement of the generally used building entrances on the open area materially aid in control and supervision.

The open campus plan permits a great deal of flexibility in the functional relationships of institutional buildings and lends a desirable informal atmosphere to institutional plants.

Buildings should be easily maintained, resistive to abuse, and so planned as to avoid hiding areas for persons or contraband. Fire-resistive construction is essential.

Doors should be so arranged to give supervisory personnel maximum view into rooms without obviously going out of their way to observe. All conference rooms should have eye-level glass panes in the doors to insure protection for male employees while doors are closed for privacy.

Security should be built in and available if it becomes necessary but should not be too evident. Security screens are satisfactory for lesser custody requirements and also serve as insect screens.

Security or strong rooms are becoming increasingly essential. Discipline and detention facilities should provide sound isolation within the area and between rooms.

Administration areas should include appropriate record space, interview rooms, and visiting areas. Above all, this area should provide enough office space for the proposed personnel.

Hospital requirements of the infirmary type are usually adequate. Single rooms and wards for above five percent of the population will be required. Isolation rooms with separate toilet facilities for both new admissions and those inmates with communicable illness are essential.

Religious facilities are essential. A chapel is recommended. However, it may be necessary to combine this with an area that also serves as a gymnasium and entertainment hall.

Gymnasiums and outdoor recreational facilities must be given more attention than in the past. Younger inmates definitely need such facilities.

Outside visiting areas have been found quite effective in some women's institutions. Facilities for informal visiting privileges are usually possible for most inmates. However, these may be used as privileged areas for those in Trustee and Honor Grade status.

The most important factor in determining fencing requirements is the location of the women's prison. Often the fence serves the purpose of keeping outsiders out to a greater degree than keeping inmates in. Fences of the industrial types are recommended by many authorities. Low fences to designate areas of activity within the prison also are often found desirable.

Colors and materials selected for inside and outside the institution are generally soft pastels and shades with stronger intermittent color accents to provide interest. When initial painting or repainting occurs, long-term inmates may be given a choice of selecting a color for their own rooms.

For landscaping the inmate areas, materials which will soften and blend the buildings to the site but which will not form visual obstructions or provide places of concealment for contraband should be chosen.

When staff housing is provided, these quarters should be as far removed as possible from the inmate area of the institution. This is necessary to insure that staff retain as much perspective as possible.

BIBLIOGRAPHY

Books

American Correctional Association: *Manual of Correctional Standards.* New York, the American Correctional Association, 1966.

U. S. Bureau of Prisons: *Recent Prison Construction 1950-1960. Supplement To Handbook of Correctional Institution Design and Construction.* 1960.

Chapter 6

THE PSYCHOPATH

Among the least understood and perhaps most destructive troublemakers in our society are the moral and emotional misfits known as psychopaths. Their warped natures frequently force them into the criminal segment of society. Even if they escape the law, they bring misery and sorrow to their fellow men far out of proportion to their numbers.

As a result of the increase in moral deterioration, the psychopathic individual is more and more coming into contact with the courts. The pressures of modern society, the lack of proper environmental supervision and training, and most of all, the breakdown of the family unit and lack of parental responsibility (largely due to unwillingness of the parents themselves to accept the responsibilities of parenthood) have helped the potential psychopath to become actual, and the actual or true congenital psychopath has little or no chance whatever to control or combat his condition. Such an individual must be made to realize that his psychopathic condition cannot be regarded as an excuse, that psychopathic or not, if he is sane, he is responsible for his acts. Such individuals must be regarded as criminals if and when they commit an offense of a criminal nature.

For several years, the term "psychopath" has been labeled "sociopath." Now the latest terminology used to designate a psychopath is that of "antisocial personality." This designation is made in the *Diagnostic and Statistical Manual of Mental Disorders,* second edition, 1968, published by the American Psychiatric Association.[1]

The designations of psychopath, sociopath, and antisocial

---

[1] Parsons, Earl: Recent changes in psychiatric diagnosis in the correctional field. *Federal Probation,* Sept., 1969, pp. 39-43.

personality are brought to the attention of nonpsychiatric personnel who use, or review reports which use, psychiatric labels, as correctional personnel must do.

For clarity, the term psychopath will be used throughout this chapter to designate the type of individual herein described.

An examination of the characteristics of the psychopath and other types of deviant behavior will be made, followed by a comparison of these personalities.

Two glaring personality deficiencies distinguish the psychopath from all other types of deviant behavior: his guiltlessness and his lovelessness.

Guilt is an important part of any well-developed conscience. When a normal person violates the moral code, he feels guilty; he feels unhappy and blames himself for the transgression. Aside from this emotional experience, guilt performs a warning function or a prevention function. People try not to transgress the moral code, for if they do they will feel guilty and unhappy— a painful experience to be avoided. Guilt is an unknown experience for the psychopathic personality with no superego. There is none of this automatic self-punishment that goes along with the commission of immoral and unethical acts. The psychopath continues to behave irresponsibly, untruthfully, insincerely, and antisocially without a shred of shame, remorse, or guilt. He may sometimes express regret and remorse for the actions and crimes which he may have perpetrated; however, these are usually mere words spoken for the effect but not really and sincerely felt.

The psychopath will cheat, lie, steal, break promises, and commit most appalling acts without remorse. He can be in deep trouble and remain calm and cool. He can be this way because he is thoroughly irresponsible and entirely unable to accept blame. Everything he does, if it makes trouble, is someone else's fault.

The absence of guilt and remorse permits the psychopath to continue his antisocial behavior indefinitely unless people in his environment or the authorities decide to exercise some control; when confronted with his lies and dishonesties, he will often try to rationalize them and give some plausible reasons for his behavior. However, these are for the most part *good*, and frequently persuasive, reasons but not the true ones.

The psychopath's warped capacity for love is so obvious that many social scientists regard it as the core of the psychopathic syndrome. The psychopathic individual is incapable of genuine love and affectional involvement with another person. To be sure, he gets involved in sex and sexual relationships, but such alliances are devoid of depth and genuineness. There is little stability in such relationships, and promiscuity is the rule. He may profess true and undying love, just as he may exhibit the external appearances of friendship. However, it is all sham and not genuine, for he flits from one "true love" to another with few qualms and no remorse.

True friendship is not within the psychopath's experience either. Although people may give him a great deal of love and affection, tolerate many of his vagaries, and exhibit nothing but good will toward him, he will not respond at all nor have in the least a similar consideration for them. He may betray them at the first opportunity and exploit their trust in him if it suits his purpose. He is incapable of making any sacrifices for or concessions to others, although others have made them in his behalf. The capacity for empathy and identification is lacking; he cannot place himself in the other fellow's shoes and imagine another person's feelings and emotional experience. Callousness and insensitivity to other people are characteristic. Other people are important to him insofar as they can be *used* by him, insofar as they are instrumental to his supreme end— self-gratification.

Antisocial behavior per se is not psychopathic, although this deviant behavior is one of the diagnostic criteria for establishing the existence of psychopathy. The psychopath shows persistent antisocial behavior without any motivation. His intelligence is undisturbed. He can think clearly, and his thinking is not distorted by illusions or hallucinations. But he has repeated, unexplained failures. He does things that appear to be done deliberately to defeat himself, for he fails to learn by experience. He can explain what course of action is correct and what is wrong, but when it comes to acting out, his judgment is markedly impaired.

The pyschopath never grows up emotionally. He grows up physically and is often well developed and attractive in appearance; he grows up intellectually inasmuch as he acquires many of the perceptual, motor, and conceptual skills which are necessary for the manipulation of the environment. However, he remains egocentric; that is, he is solely concerned with the fulfillment of his own needs and wishes *immediately*. Since, like the small child, he can suffer no delay or postponement, he becomes extremely frustrated when his desires are thwarted by the environment. Likewise, he proceeds impulsively to do and get what he wishes without consideration for others. And when he does, there are no pangs of conscience to bother him.

Unlike the young child, however, the psychopath has developed and matured physically and has acquired many important skills which he can employ in the manipulation of his environment. Thus, he may bring many of these aspects of maturity to the service of his childish needs and impulse satisfaction; or in the case of frustration, he may use them against other people who are in his way. Such situations often constitute the dangers to society and to ordered living that are embodied in the psychopath.

The psychopath cannot learn from his experiences, for the capacity of self-control has never developed properly. Thus he may go on committing the very acts for which he was punished on one or more occasions previously. Past experience somehow does not affect his future behavior. The infantile needs are strong, the control apparatus is weak; the result is that behavior remains governed by the former, unguided by the latter.

Life, for the psychopath, is a hit-or-miss affair. It consists of a series of episodes of impulsive acts which are not instrumental in long-range planning for a career, in the achievement of socially desirable goals, or in the attainment of stability of social, economic, and emotional status. Although he may at times resolve to follow a certain plan for his future, he fails in the actual realization of such a program. Too many immediate and temporary lures dissuade him from his chosen long-range goal; he never gets where he allegedly wishes to go, for the gratification of the immediate need and the impulsive reactions hinder such achievements. Even his crimes are rarely planned. He will rob a store on the spur of the moment, rather than after careful planning.

The psychopath does not hold onto a job for any length of time, although he may be quite successful at it. Sudden outbursts against fellow workers, manager, boss, customers; flagrant manipulation of the truth and other kinds of dishonesty; unreliability and lack of a sense of responsibility are all part of the picture of an unstable and shifting employment picture.

Sex for the psychopath is primarily a matter of physical contact, uncomplicated by the emotion of love. Sexual activities are casual affairs without emotional involvement.

A psychopath is a person without a conscience, without the capacity to experience guilt, who is incapable of adhering to the rules and mores of society, who is impulsive and emotionally immature and egocentric, who is incapable of genuine interpersonal relationships, of long-range planning and considered anticipation of the future.

THE NEUROTIC

The neurotic feels intense anxiety and inner conflict. He is continually under tension, chronically dissatisfied, and often rigid and inhibited. The neurotic attempts to solve this conflict in a variety of ways—by repression, by regression, or by other protective mechanisms. He may develop a phobia, an obsession, an hysteric symptom, or he may revert to severe anxiety attacks if all defenses fail. He tries to assuage his inner disturbance with unrealistic means, but he never severs his contacts with reality.

The "Acting-out" Neurotic

Like other neurotics, the "acting-out' neurotic feels chronic inner conflict. However, instead of repressing his feelings, the "acting-out" neurotic tries to resolve the conflict through antisocial behavior. When anxiety and tension increase unbearably, he explodes into aggressive attacks. His behavior stems from compulsion, hysteria, and depression, which can be appeased only through action.

THE PSYCHOTIC

Psychotics all possess a serious loss of contact with reality. They withdraw from frustration and create a private delusional world. Self-reference pervades their thinking, and hallucinations surround them. Sometimes the psychotic undergoes extreme depression and sometimes an exalted grandiosity. He may alter between stupor and frenzy and often has delusions of persecution. The psychotic often feels intense guilt or anxiety.

THE "NORMAL" CRIMINAL DEVIANT

Criminal behavior is that behavior which is defined by criminal law as being criminal. Any act which, by omission or commission, runs counter to the criminal law could be defined as a crime or criminal behavior in the legal sense. A great deal of criminal and delinquent behavior is behavior of the moment; it is extemporaneous. Crimes of anger and passion largely come within this category, where there is no background which adequately explains the violent reaction except the upset of the moment. Many offenders just drift into an act of violation or are precipitated into it by fast-rising events of the situation over which they have had very little control. They are not disorganized or demoralized persons but fairly well adjusted individuals in their particular milieu. When a child is reared in a criminal environment by criminal parents, he is likely to develop both a criminal ego and a criminal superego.[2]

COMPARISONS

Benjamine Karpman has made a chart illustrating differentials in neurosis, psychosis, and psychopathy. In the chart, he divides psychosis into two types; schizophrenia and manic-depressive. He also divides psychopathy into two types; symptomatic psychopathy (which we call "acting-out" neurosis) and primary psychopathy (true psychopathy). The following comparisons are taken from Karpman's chart.[3]

---

[2] MacDonald, John M.: *Psychiatry and the Criminal.* Springfield, Thomas, 1958, p. 15.

[3] Karpman, Benjamine: The structure of neurosis. *Archives of Criminal Psychodynamics,* Fall, 1961.

Tender Attachments

Neurosis. Marked emotional dependence on others.

Schizophrenia. Is capable of tender attachments but also fears them. Is too absorbed in own fantasy life to maintain or establish tender attachments, which are felt more inwardly than expressed outwardly.

Manic-depressive. Overly social, but keeps away from close attachments because of inability to manage them emotionally—tries to keep his emotional life intact and away from others.

Acting-out neurotic. Few real attachments. Tends to attract dependent persons whom he exploits. Large element of hostility in close attachments. Attaches self to anyone he can seduce to supply needs. Often underlying hostility to those who help him. Parasitic attachment.

Psychopath. Does not have capacity for tender attachments. Desires to dominate only. Simulates attachments in order to prey on others. Parasitic, predatory attachment only.

Ambivalence

Neurosis. Extremely ambivalent in emotions and behavior, resulting in emotional confusion and indecision. Parallel feelings of love, hostility, self-sacrifice; and callous egotism, over-scrupulousness, and extravagance, etc.

Schizophrenia. Basically ambivalent, opposing emotions can exist side by side, greater separation of opposing behavior tends to follow one or other at different times rather than rapid alternation and fusion as in neurotic. Marked effect on intellect as well as emotions.

Manic-depressive. Ambivalence most marked, fluctuation of mood and emotion in manic phase.

Acting-out neurotic. Ambivalence deeply buried and usual emotional state shows little ambivalence due to dominant concern with purely selfish, immediate interests.

Psychopath. Not at all ambivalent. Quick changes as outside situation changes in his search for satisfaction of the moment.

Tension States

Neurosis. Accumulation of tension since neurotics cannot adequately discharge or release emotions. Extreme stress and strain because of inner conflicts. Accumulated tension results in emotional outbursts or overflows into substitute forms of behavior. Means of discharge sought immediately, or recourse may be taken to alcohol and drugs.

Schizophrenia. Long-term accumulation of tension leading to psychotic episodes, sometimes very violent, of almost random discharge of energy.

Manic-depressive. Long-term accumulation of tension. Tension rises quickly but cannot be tolerated, immediate release sought.

Psychopath. No accumulation of tension. Tension rises quickly in response to instinctual urges but is immediately discharged.

Inadequacy

Neurosis. Strong feelings of inadequacy stemming from feelings of inferiority.

Schizophrenia. Strong feelings of inadequacy contribute to the retreat from reality.

Manic-depressive. Strong feelings of inadequacy leading alternately to attempts to overcompensate and complete abandonment of the effort.

Acting-out neurotic. Feels inadequate in respect to social demands, abandons any attempts to fulfill social obligations—feels adequate only in predatory activities.

Psychopath. No feelings of inadequacy; what is feasible is only criterion.

Anxiety

Neurosis. Anxiety states easily developed. Always fearful and apprehensive.

Schizophrenia. Intense anxiety precedes withdrawal from reality. Schizophrenic retreats into depression or dissociates emotion from the situation, resulting in either a lack of emotional response or in an inappropriate response to the situation.

Manic-depressive. Anxiety appropriate to situation but very exaggerated in manic state. Depressed state follows when anxiety and guilt become too strong or mania fails to accomplish its intended purpose.

Acting-out neurotic. Little anxiety from unconscious or emotional states, responds with fear to perceived threat. Hostility instead of anxiety.

Psychopath. No anxiety from unconscious or emotional causes, only fear at perceived threat to own well-being.

Hostility

Neurosis. Unconscious hate becomes a source of generalized hostility. Type of hostility reaction and method of handling it depend on individual development. Usually displaced onto symbolic representation of source of original feelings of hate or at times turned against self.

Schizophrenia. Depending on type of schizophrenic reaction, hostility either directed toward self or may explode in violent aggression against others, usually as symbolic representations of source. Often becomes dissociated from external situation and does not appear present when situation should evoke it.

Manic-depressive. Hostility strongly suppressed. Released in manic phase in irritability, anger, or through reaction formation by overfriendly feelings and altruism. In depressive phase, directed against self.

Acting-out neurotic. Strong generalized hostility crowds out anxiety or depression. Hostility is dominant background emotion and often leads to criminal behavior.

Psychopath. Specific hate and rage when frustrated rather than generalized hostility. Quickly disappears when need is satisfied. When unsatisfied, may lead to aggressive criminal acts.

Sex Life

Neurosis. Sex life characterized by variability, deviations from the norm. Most often heterosexual but with deviate practices. Neurotic blocking often results in homosexuality, exhibitionism, voyeurism, etc. Strong sex urges.

Schizophrenia. Conservative sex life. Even normal sex seems excessive. In psychotic states with loss of control, many deviations from normal and open sex behavior of all kinds. Weak sex urge.

Manic-depressive. Prior to onset, sex activity less than normal. In manic phase, overactive, diverse sexual behavior. In depressive phrase, sex expression reduced or lacking.

Acting-out neurotic. Great variability. Little affectional element. Hostility often expressed in sex behavior.

Psychopath. Great variability, many deviations from normal sex used for pleasure or as tension-relieving device, no affectional element. Any mode of sex expression used, since there are no inhibitions.

Conscience and Guilt Feelings

Neurosis. Sensitive conscience, strong guilt feelings. Inability to tolerate guilt feeling leads to expiative behavior.

Schizophrenia. Extremely sensitive conscience, rigid and over-strict. Constant struggle. Inability to effect workable compromises with conscience leads to breakdown.

Manic-depressive. Repression of guilt feelings through great activity in manic state; overwhelming sense of guilt in depression.

Acting-out neurotic. Very little sense of guilt; uncovered with great difficulty.

Psychopath. No guilt feelings.

Guilt-produced Behavior, Social and Antisocial

Neurosis. Defensive lying, tendency to exaggerate and evade facts. Variety of private expiatory or propitiatory measures. Guilt-produced tension seeks relief in forbidden acts and produces still more guilt; a vicious circle.

Schizophrenia. Overreaction to guilt feelings. Highly symbolic criminal acts to destroy cause of guilt. Loss of control and failure of repression results in hostile aggressive acts. Guilt is dissociated from guilt-producing behavior.

Manic-depressive. Overreaction to guilt feelings. Highly symbolic criminal acts to destroy cause of guilt. Loss of control and failure of repression results in hostile aggressive acts. Guilt is dissociated from guilt-producing behavior.

Acting-out neurotic. Little guilt-produced behavior and very little self-punishment. Hostility replaces guilt feelings.

Psychopath. No real guilt-produced behavior. Pseudoneurotic guilt from need to conform for own protection. Fear rather than guilt. No self-punishment.

Judgment

Neurosis. Judgment strongly affected by emotions, particularly hostile emotions which result in antisocial and criminal acts.

Schizophrenia. Judgment strongly affected by emotions, intellectual functions distorted or disrupted.

Acting-out neurotic. Judgment itself is bad because of prevalence of hostility, lack of guilt, need for sensual indulgence, and immaturity.

Psychopath. Judgment itself is bad, immature, and naive, based only on primitive relations or on "sets" resulting from previous experience.

Lack of Responsibility

Neurosis. Neurotic trends basically asocial, antisocial or even criminal. Emotional pressures lead to lack of control and lack of responsibility. Criminal acts have only the value of symptomatic symbolic acts, a result of the neurotic condition.

Schizophrenia. Originally very responsible, forced to abandon all responsibility as psychosis develops. Antisocial acts result either from loss of conscious control or are highly symbolic.

Manic-depressive. Originally very responsible, disturbances in emotions and thought process destroy responsibility.

Acting-out neurotic. Very little sense of responsibility to others.

Psychopath. No sense of responsibility to others.

Antisocial Acts

Neurosis. Antisocial acts usually of one particular type which has symbolic meaning for the individual neurotic. In other areas, the neurotic is usually honest and trustworthy.

Schizophrenia. Two types: (a) Highly symbolic acts or crimes related to cause of the psychosis; may involve considerable planning and premeditation. (b) Impulsive acts or crimes due to lack of control.

Manic-depressive. Two types: (a) Highly symbolic acts or crimes related to causes of psychosis. May involve considerable planning and premeditation. (b) Impulsive acts or crimes due to lack of control.

Acting-out neurotic. Antisocial reactions dominate behavior so as to cause strong resemblance to primary psychopath. Antisocial and criminal acts have elements of symbolic behavior.

Psychopath. Asocial rather than antisocial. No inner restrictions or controls to prevent antisocial or criminal behavior. Responds only to external controls. Criminal for gain or to remove obstacles to his desires. Opportunistic.

Ambition

Neurosis. Normal ambitions plus compensatory strivings. Level of aspiration too high (characteristically) in relation to level of achievement.

Schizophrenia. Impossibly high levels of aspiration in relation to possibilities of achievement. After development of psychosis, ambition may lose all relation to reality or may disappear.

Manic-depressive. Impossibly high levels of aspiration in relation to possibilities of achievement. In manic phase may be completely unrealistic, in depressive phase may disappear entirely, leading to suicide.

Acting-out neurotic. No real level of aspiration, ambitions closely related to particular individual's pattern for satisfying needs. Fantasy goals unrelated to individual's capacities.

Psychopath. Ambition dependent entirely upon pattern he develops to satisfy his needs and desires. No real level of aspirations, lives only in present; future goals consist only in wealth and power to serve his desires.

FURTHER COMPARISONS

In *The Psychology of Sex Offenders,* Ellis and Brancale have compared the psychopath with neurotic and psychotic personalities in general, as well as in the area of sex.[4]

Unlike the true psychopath, who not only repetitiously commits antisocial acts but also has little or no guilt or effect

---

[4] Ellis, Albert, and Brancale, Ralph. *The Psychology of Sex Offenders.* Springfield, Thomas, 1956.

concerning these acts and is not disturbed by his continual aggressions against society, the neurotic knows that he is doing wrong and feels some degree of guilt, often considerable, about his misdeeds.

The true psychopath normally tends to commit several or many kinds of antisocial acts. He will steal, fight, and act in a sexually impulsive manner. He reacts to all phases of social conduct with unbridled, primitive aggression and immature drive. On the other hand, the neurotic may only steal or assault others or engage in illegal sex acts, or he may especially engage in some specific type of antisocial behavior which may serve as a symbolic or particularized outlet for his neurosis.

Because a neurotic is overinhibited, he feels compulsively forced to break through his inhibitory shell with antisocial drivers. The psychopath, on the other hand, is a relatively ego-integrated individual who does a good many self-centered, socially prohibited acts impulsively and recklessly just because he wants to. Where the neurotic is basically overrestrained, the psychopath is underrestrained, and where the neurotic is overtly or unconsciously filled with anxiety, the psychopath feels no anxiety.

The term "sexual psychopath" has been used erroneously to describe all manner of sex offenders. When accurately used, the term should apply to an offender who has considerable self-integration and ability to stand up against others and who has adequate sexual drive, but who disobeys both society's sexual as well as its nonsexual laws. This offender will often sadistically attack a woman who refuses his favors, will have sex relations with young children, or will engage in homosexual activities. On the other hand, the neurotically deviated sex offenders are often intensely insecure and nonintegrated individuals who have never gained much poise, social courage, or emotional stability and who are often inhibited and impotent not only in their sex drives but in most aspects of their personality.

Two of the most common types of sex offenders are the compulsive neurotic and the schizoid or borderline psychotic offender. They give the appearance of hypersexuality and over-impulsivity when actually they are low-sexed and under-impulsive.[5] The compulsive neurotic, an inwardly inhibited person, abnormally holds himself in most of the time, and he actually behaves in a compulsive manner.

The schizoid or borderline psychotic also may normally hold himself in sexually (and otherwise), but his eventual outbursts of sexuality tend to take on a totally unrealistic and bizarre pattern which may appear to be almost without motive. While the neurotic's explosion of sexuality will normally be of a physically harmless nature (homosexuality or exhibitionism), the psychotic's sexual outbursts may be so bizarre as to lead to physically violent sex acts (sadistic assault or homicidal rape).[6]

Both the neurotic's and the psychotic's sex acts are compulsive rather than impulsive. In fact, the psychotic's sex behavior is often so compulsive that he is totally unable to control himself, is literally driven by his terrible underlying anxiety to thoroughly reckless acts, shows little or no regard for safeguarding himself from the consequences of his compulsions, and consequently is usually apprehended for his sex offenses. While it might appear that the psychotic's sex drives are forcing him to violate sex laws, the true fact is that his basic compelling drives are probably largely of a nonsexual, and more general, nature. His general sickness may force him to act in a sexually (as well as otherwise) sick manner.[7]

Man's basic sex impulses are enormously influenced by his cultural upbringing. While the power of man's biological sex drives is not to be minimized, it is to a large extent controllable; and the direction of these drives, whether autosexual, homosexual, or heterosexual, seems to be almost entirely a matter of learning rather than innate instinct.[8]

MANAGEMENT OF THE PSYCHOPATH IN PRISON

The definitions of the psychopath and the comparisons made between the psychopath and other types of deviant behavior do not tell us how to manage the psychopath in prison; however,

---

[5] *Ibid.*, p. 40.
[6] *Ibid.*, p. 44.
[7] *Ibid.*, p. 44.
[8] *Ibid.*, p. 127.

before we can manage him, we must be able to understand him.

Roger D. Kalina presented a paper at the American Correctional Conference in Denver in 1960 that will help you to identify the psychopaths in your prison, and which makes suggestions on how to manage them. This information is important for *all* prison personnel to know.

MANAGEMENT OF THE PSYCHOPATH[9]

ROGER K. KALINA, M.D.

Everyone talks about the psychopath. Unfortunately, everyone who makes trouble is labeled "psychopath" regardless of why he presents problems.

The genuine psychopath has been classified by many definitions. These definitions, in addition to being numerous, are frequently long and complex and tremendously varied, and do not help much in the understanding of the psychopath.

Before we can manage this individual, we have to understand him.

Let us consider how a psychopath behaves. It is his behavior that furnishes the diagnostic criteria for establishing the existence of psychopathy.

1. Psychopaths have *undisturbed intelligence.* They can think clearly and their thinking is not distorted. Their thoughts are not disorganized by delusions or hallucinations. Intelligence may be well above average.

2. These people, who may even have superior intelligence, show repeated, *unexplained failures.* They are temporarily successful in school, business, etc., and then repeatedly fail in one enterprise after another.

3. Psychopaths show an absence of *neurotic anxiety.* They are not neurotic. The absence of anxiety or concern over their activities is remarkable. Psychopaths can be in deep trouble and remain the unconcerned, calm, and cool man or woman who is much admired by cons, television fans, and other immature individuals. They feel no guilt.

4. They can be this way because the psychopath is *thoroughly irresponsible* and *entirely unable to accept blame.* They never feel guilty. Everything they do, if it makes trouble, is someone

---

[9] Kalina, Roger K.: Management of the psychopath. *Proceedings of the Ninetieth Annual Congress of Correction of the American Correction Association,* Denver, Colorado, August 28th-September 2nd, 1960, pp. 268-271.

else's fault. They can commit crimes, desert their families, etc., without concern, because it's never their fault. If you are confronted with only one instance of such behavior, they can frequently convince you that they are unfortunate, misunderstood individuals. But they repeat themselves so often that you begin to suspect that you are just one more of us who has been taken in by a psychopath.

5. These people show *persistent antisocial behavior without any motivation.* They have money and write hot checks, abandon happy families, and they do things that appear to be done deliberately to defeat themselves.

6. They have a *marked disregard for the truth.* They can differentiate truth from untruth, but for many it seems easier to lie than to speak the truth.

7. *They fail to learn by experience.* They repeat over and over the things that get them into trouble. In theory, they can explain what course of action is correct and what is wrong: but when it comes to acting out, their *judgment is markedly impaired.* Any of us may use poor judgment on an occasion; but the psychopath does it repeatedly in spite of his intelligence.

8. Psychopaths have an *incapacity for deep and enduring personal attachments.* They may profess profound love and affection and demonstrate it for a time but it never lasts. They usually eventually walk out on a family and associates—hurting them deeply in the process and typically blaming anyone but themselves.

Their sexual attachments are superficial and for pleasure. They experiment with perversions to attempt to increase sexual gratification. There is no feeling of guilt or thought of wrong. And if you listen to them they will explain how someone else conned them into the perverse activity.

Psychopaths *rarely commit suicide.* They will often make gestures that are impressive. Psychopaths can "suffer beautifully." Their suicidal gestures usually have some motivation. They elicit sympathy. They get attention—our women usually cut themselves in the evening so someone has to be called out to sew them up. They do it early enough to get a full night's sleep. Thus, with one act they often get attention, sympathy, and sedation.

After speaking of all these undesirable traits of the psychopath, we must never lose sight of the fact that their behavior can be exemplary. They can be the type of person we would most like to have as our friends. But they can't maintain normal social adjustments.

How to change a true psychopath is not known (to me or anyone else I know). How to manage them is at best a trying problem.

First, we know they can't be trusted. Sometimes circumstances force us to put them in positions of trust. If possible, have a replacement or substitute available. They have a special predilection for letting you down when you need them most.

Don't get upset by their behavior. If they know they can provoke anxiety in you—force you to lose your temper or become upset in any way—they will just persist all the more in their behavior.

Don't go out of your way to make things satisfactory for the psychopath; don't favor him or sympathize with him to keep him from causing trouble. Favoring the psychopath just loses you the cooperation of your reasonable charges.

As stated repeatedly, the psychopath is frequently in trouble and he loves company in trouble. They will lie and provoke fights between others (they are usually too intelligent to involve themselves in physical violence). They will threaten, usually to get a lawyer, to write to the warden, a senator, etc., to scare you. Unfortunately, so many people are taken in by these individuals that they can cause trouble. Don't be afraid of them. Their persistent psychopathic behavior will reveal them.

The psychopath's life is a life of trouble. Locking him up won't change him. It only keeps him out of circulation and out of the hair of the public.

Prison just confines the trouble, as well as the psychopath, to the prison. The trouble is ours—expect it. His behavior will be excellent for a time, but keep always in mind that it's going to change.

Be calm about it—at least look calm and act calm.

As long as you remain in command of any situation the psychopath creates, you, and not he, is in charge. Understand and watch him and his behavior, or the psychopath may take charge without you knowing it.

Now, instead of a lot of "don'ts"—specifically what do you have to know and do, to manage a psychopath.

First, know who your psychopaths are. You know what characteristics they need to qualify. Check their records of their lifetime behavior. It will be obvious which of your inmates are psychopaths.

Expect these people to make trouble for no apparent reason.

When you listen to them, remember they can lie without concern.

Watch them closely. Remember that in spite of their intelligence, they often work against themselves. How else can they get credit for their acts if they aren't detected?

It won't be easy. It requires constant vigilance.

Treat them without favors or special consideration—and without condemnation. To condemn them simply gives them justification for their behavior.

The less special attention or consideration they receive (or know they receive) the less trouble they will be. To give them importance makes them feel they have to act out their importance—and make trouble.

When you encounter the psychopath, don't give in to discouragement and frustration.

Psychopaths are only people. They aren't superior. They have nothing extra that we don't have. Their difference is in what they lack, not how they excel.

The better you know your individual psychopath, the better you can manage him, with a minimum of trouble.

Know your psychopath and you will manage him.

SUMMARY

Everyone talks about the psychopath. Unfortunately, everyone who makes trouble is labeled "psychopath" regardless of why she presents problems.

Behavior such as the following is the key to identifying the psychopath.

1. The psychopath has undisturbed intelligence.
2. She shows repeated, unexplained failures.
3. She feels no guilt.
4. She is thoroughly irresponsible and entirely unable to accept blame.
5. She shows persistent antisocial behavior without any motivation.
6. She has a marked disregard for the truth.
7. She fails to learn by experience.
8. She has an incapacity for deep and enduring personal attachments.

The psychopath in prison can be managed in the following ways:

1. Don't trust her.
2. Don't get upset by her behavior.
3. Don't favor her.
4. Don't be afraid of her.
5. Be calm.
6. Remain in command.
7. Know who your psychopaths are.

8. Remember that they lie without concern.

9. Watch them closely; they often work against themselves.

10. Don't give them special attention or importance.

The better you know your individual psychopath, the better you will manage her.

BIBLIOGRAPHY

Books

De River, J. Paul: *Crime and the Sexual Psychopath*. Springfield, Thomas, 1958.

Ellis, Albert, and Brancale, Ralph: *The Psychology of Sex Offenders*. Springfield, Thomas, 1956.

Macdonald, John M.: *Psychiatry and the Criminal*. Springfield, Thomas, 1958.

McCord, William, and McCord, Joan: *Psychopathy and Delinquency*. New York, Grune, 1956.

Reckless, Walter C.: *The Crime Problem*. New York, Appelton, 1950.

Toch, Hans: *Legal and Criminal Psychology*. New York, Holt, 1961.

Articles and Periodicals

Kalina, Roger K.: Management of the Psychopath. *Proceedings of the Ninetieth Annual Congress of Correction of the American Correctional Association,* Denver, Colorado, 1960.

Karpman, Benjamine (Ed.): *Archives of Criminal Psychodynamics, Special Psychopathy Issue*. Washington, D. C., 1961.

Karpman, Benjamine (Ed.): The structure of neuroses. *Archives of Criminal Psychodynamics*. Fall 1961.

Parsons, Earl: Recent changes in psychiatric diagnoses in the correctional field. *Federal Probation,* September, 1969, pp. 39-43.

Chapter 7

BABIES IN PRISON

THE PROBLEM

A PROBLEM UNIQUE to women's prisons is the unresolved question of what to do with pregnant inmates, the babies born while the mother is incarcerated, and minor children of inmate-mothers.

A significant number of minor children are affected by the imprisonment of the mother. In any women's prison, more than half of the inmates will be mothers of minor children.

When separation results from the mother's incarceration because she has been judged guilty of committing a felony, the consequences for the children take on dramatic and troubling dimensions that may not be present in other separation circumstances. Aside from such considerations as who—if anyone—is available to keep the family together and/or to provide the children with material and emotional care, there are special and particular elements to take into account such as the following: Are the moral and social attitudes of the family members and of the community towards a person who has committed a crime harsher with regard to the woman offender? What will be the nature and frequency of continuing contact, if any, between the imprisoned mother and her children—*will* there be, *can* there be, *should* there be visits to the prison, an exchange of letters or presents, consideration of the mother's wishes or ideas in planning with respect to the children? What rights does she retain as a parent? What stigma, if any, do the mother or father or children attach to her imprisonment? What is the effect upon the present and future functioning of the children?

Ramifications of the Problem

The family, especially the mother-child relationships, is viewed by the psychoanalyst as the matrix within which the child's basic personality and character are developed. The research in psychoanalysis, and social psychology has shown that childhood relationships play a paramount role in the formation of adult personality. Research also indicates a strong link between early emotional deprivation (parental conflict, cruelty, erratic punishment, and particularly, parental neglect) and the emergence of a psychopathic syndrome.

Bowlby,[1] for example, considers the effects of the child's lack of opportunity to form an attachment to a mother figure during the first three years of life, the effects of deprivation (i.e. of attention, contact, and affection) for at least three, and probably more than six, months during the first three or four years of the child's life, and the effects of changes from one mother-figure to another during the same period. He suggests that such experiences lead to emotional withdrawal and isolation of the child, with an inability to develop loving ties with children or adults, faulty character formation, with a lack of conscience or guilt; feelings of violence and anger resulting in acute conflict, anxiety, and depressions which may be expressed in aggressively bad or legally delinquent behavior, or which ultimately may lead to suicide; and becoming a parent who lacks the capacity to truly care for her children.

Among the most definitive works was that done by Bender.[2] In her clinical work at New York's Bellevue Hospital, Bender examined hundreds of children psychopaths. She found similar personality symptoms in all: diffuse impulsiveness, an inability to feel guilt, manipulation of morality without emotional meaning, and an "inability to identify themselves in a relationship with other people." Furthermore, her study indicated that all the psychopathic children had experienced emotional deprivation, neglect, or discontinuous affectional relationships. Bender believed that early emotional starvation, particularly during the first three years, leads to psychopathy. "We know that the critical time," she wrote, "is the first three years, especially the

---

[1] Bowlby, John: *Child Care And The Growth of Love.* London, Whitefriars, 1953.

[2] McCord, William, and McCord, Joan: *The Psychopath.* Princeton, Van Nostrand, 1964, p. 75.

first year; any significant break in parent relationships or any period of deprivation under five years may be sufficient to produce this personality defect."

Zalba,[3] in 1960, studied the need for specialized child welfare services among forty inmate-mothers and expectant mothers at the California Institution for Women. It was her position that while many inmate-mothers had personal histories which raised serious doubts as to their abilities to provide adequate mothering for their children, they did express interest and concern about their children (and these expressions were strongly supported by institutional culture). Thus the mothers might be amenable, while incarcerated, to offers of child welfare services that would help resolve the future mother-child relationships. She stated that the inmate-mothers and their children had the same needs for child welfare services as other mothers and children, but child welfare agencies tended to think primarily in terms of terminating the formal relationships of inmate-mother and child, usually without adequate knowledge of the mother's circumstances, institutional program of treatment, and probable length of confinement.

The most numerous and severe problems which were evident throughout a study[4] made of the psychological needs of women in a correctional institution had to do with the individual herself, and they involved such things as what the psychologist has referred to as self-acceptance, self-understanding, and self-realization. It is the opinion of the authors that the immediate family unit is more an inextricable part of the adult female than it is of the male and that when she is separated from that unit through commitment to a correctional institution, the problems in this area are often quite acute. The opinions of inmates involved in this study rated the family adjustment problems as being only second to that of the personal and self-adjustment of the individual.

------

[3] Zalba, Serapio: *Women Prisoners and Their Families.* Los Angeles, Delmar, 1964, p. 6.

[4] Cassell, Russell N., and Van Corst, Robert B.: Psychological needs of women in a correctional institution. *American Journal of Correction,* January-February, 1961, pp. 22-24.

THE OBJECTIVE

The control, by the prison, over the range of the inmate's behavior and choices, is reacted to by the inmates by regression to less mature behavior. Typically this behavior of the inmates takes the form of dependency—wanting others to perform tasks and take responsibilities for them—and of complaints about the services provided for them. The consequence is antithetical to the goal of the institution to treat the inmates in such a way as to make them increasingly responsible so that upon their release to the community their behavior will be more adequate and socially acceptable.

The primary objective of this proposal is to help each prison formulate certain policies, procedures, and services to meet the needs of women inmates and their families. The following basic questions must be taken into account: What happens to women who are pregnant at the time they are committed to an institution? Where are the babies born? What happens to the minor children of a mother convicted of a felony and sent to prison? Who cares for the children? Who supports them? What agencies provide social welfare services for the family? To what extent are the services coordinated? What is the role of the mother while she is in prison? Will she maintain contact with her children through visits, letters, and presents? Will she participate in decisions regarding arrangements for the care and training of her children during her incarceration and in planning for their future?

Focusing the attention of client-families on the mother and her children does not deny the importance of the father. However, no father is available in many of the homes.

ANALYSIS

Virtually no research has been reported on women in prison, although there have been studies of family separations occurring under many other circumstances.

A study[5] was conducted at the California Institution for

---

[5] Zalba, Serapio R.: *Women Prisoners and Their Families.* Los Angeles, Delmar, 1964.

Women, the largest women's prison in the United States, under the joint sponsorship and financing of the California Department of Social Welfare and the Department of Corrections.

This study, completed in 1964, was designed to increase understanding of the problems of interagency involvement in cases where the mothers of minor children are incarcerated.

Through the study of this research done at the California Institution for Women, certain problems common to all women's prisons can be identified and therefore can be dealt with in a more realistic manner.

Analysis of Families

The analysis of the data collected concerning the families disclosed, among other things, that the inmate-mother's own rehabilitation and adjustment are sharply affected by her maternal role and her continuing relationship relative to her children. Unless there is clarification and stabilization of the role she is to play in the rearing of her children, she will be faced with demands and crises that adversely affect her ability to utilize the institutional program or successfully complete parole.

Despite the fact that many inmates had been inadequate or disinterested in performing the mother role before imprisonment, the institutional culture strongly supports expressions of concern about one's children. As part of their response to institutional culture, some inmate-mothers make unrealistic plans to take their children back upon release. Once paroled, they may not act upon the plans; but if they do, the results could be questionable removal of children from households they had come to know as home. Such precipitous movement of children could detract from the mother's potential for parole success, as well as from the children's chances for a stable social and emotional adjustment.

Among the cases studied in this project, there were few indications of family-oriented planning, especially for the future of the children. The adults responsible for taking care of the children in the absence of the mother seemed to prefer to avoid thinking about the future. When planning was evident, it seldom involved the mother nor was she consulted about it. Sometimes agencies or family members made necessary and realistic plans for long-term placement of the children away from the mother.

The mother may not have been consulted because of her lack of interest or involvement with the children. Nevertheless, many emotionally deprived women at the institution could not let go of their children, and help in becoming ready to do so generally was not available. The study disclosed the care required to resolve the feelings of the inmate-mother regarding separation from her children in the future. Her feelings of deprivation as a prisoner may be imputed by her to her separation from her children; this, then, militates against her acceptance of plans for long-term custody by others. Her negative feelings about such plans may result in her sabotaging sound arrangements made for her children.

The field study offered support to the conclusion that a child who remained with relatives during his mother's absence maintained a greater sense of belonging and identity than did a child in foster care. The interviews with the inmate-mother brought out the fact that the inmate's family of orientation—her own parents, aunts, uncles, etc.—despite its problems, was a resource with considerable potential for supportive help to her and her children during and following her incarceration.

Some children and caretakers had specific unmet needs for which services currently existed in the community. In many cases, they did not know where to obtain the needed help; for them the community resources were latent instead of real.

Analysis of the Agencies

The analysis of the data collected concerning the agencies disclosed that about half of the inmate's families were financially dependent upon the county welfare departments and the receipt of Aid to Families with Dependent Children. It was found that when more than one agency worked with the same family, inter-agency contact was minimal. Such contacts as were made were concerned primarily with matters of administrative procedures and eligibility.

It was evident that caseworkers were not clear about their own agency policy regarding the sharing of casework information with other agencies, nor did the agencies included in this study generally have alternative written policy directions. There were, in fact, some situations wherein workers of some of these agencies had advised other agencies that it was contrary to their agency policy to share casework data contained in their official files. There also was little evidence that workers understood the policies or functions of other agencies.

Sharing of casework information was practically nonexistent either between public welfare and/or juvenile probation departments with the California Institution for Women or between the Institution and public welfare or juvenile probation departments. The California Institution for Women worker received inadequate information both about the inmate's current family situation in the community and her preinstitutional performance in her family. On the other hand, neither county public welfare departments nor the women's parole division (the state parole agency supervising the offenders on parole after their release from the California Institution for Women) received adequate information about the inmate-mother's institutional performance or her postrelease plans. Both as a *result* of this breakdown in communication and as a *cause* of it, neither the institution nor the agencies in the community regularly undertook a plan for the future based on an awareness of the interdependent nature of relationships in the family; that is, that plans for one member or family unit affected the plans of the others. Yet the most striking need manifest among the families studied was for stabilization of the children's living situations so that all family members might begin to make long-term adjustments based on healthier parent-child relationships.

This failure to share information and accordingly, to develop appropriate plans for the future, constituted a vicious cycle. Without adequate information that, in fact, often was obtainable from other agencies, workers in all of the concerned agencies found it difficult to plan realistically. And unless and until they had initiated such planning, it would be difficult to decide what kind of information they required from the other agencies involved. Plans that were made by an agency were seldom communicated to the other relevant agencies or coordinated with the latter's planning. The planning that did exist was not essentially *family-oriented*. Plans were made for individuals or for groups of individuals, rather than for family groups.

Prerelease plans were required for inmates prior to appearances before the Women's Board of Trustees for parole consideration, but these plans usually were made *by* the inmate, rather than *with* her. Also, they did not take into account information about the current reality situation confronting her in the community—spouse, children, employment, etc.—which would have enabled the institution's worker to participate meaningfully in the planning.

Although both the parole agents and the public welfare workers had responsibilities for making decisions affecting the possible reunion of the mother and her children or other child-care arrangements, they were not usually involved in the formulation of parole plans. In many cases the public welfare workers learned of the mother's release only upon seeing her in the home during a home visit.

The reverse often was true of planning relative to the children. Even though many of the mothers had been less than responsible or adequate while living in the community, they were nevertheless in a position to sabotage otherwise sound and realistic plans for child care. It seems imperative, for the sake of the children *and* the mother, that joint planning be initiated and carried through with agency, as well as client, participation.

RECOMMENDATIONS

Ideally the State Department of Welfare and the State Department of Corrections should develop an interdepartmental guide, setting forth state policy and procedure for the sharing of information among county welfare departments, state correctional institutions, and state parole offices.

Realistically, the women's prison may have to be the instigator of such a program.

Assuming that the prison, because of its concern with the

inmate and her total family situation, takes the lead in developing cohesive family-oriented planning, several areas of concern are brought to the readers attention.

Guardianship Services

There should be the provision of guardianship services to insure that the children of incarcerated mothers are adequately protected. If a state has this guardianship service, all minor children of arrested mothers should automatically come under its care and custody. These guardianship services can be administered by the Juvenile Court.

All actions must be based on some statutory empowerment.

A California law that makes provision for the children of female inmates might be used as a guide by other prisons in formulating new legislation. This is California Penal Code, 1947, Revised Section 3401:

> Admission of Children of Inmates; Age Limit; Period of Retention; Subsequent Care; Temporary Liberation of Prisoners for Childbirth Purposes; Liability for Expense. If any woman received by or committed to said institution (California Institution for Women) has a child under two years of age, or gives birth to a child while an inmate of said institution, such child may be admitted to, and retained in, said institution until it reaches the age of two years, at which time said board may arrange for its care elsewhere; and provided further, that at its discretion in exceptional cases said board may retain such child for a longer period of time.
>
> Any woman inmate who would give birth to a child during her term of imprisonment may be temporarily taken to a hospital outside the prison for the purposes of childbirth, and the charge for hospital and medical care shall be charged against the funds allocated to the institution. The board shall provide for the care of any children so born and shall pay for their care until suitably placed.[6]

Keeping Babies in Prison

With a law that makes provision for keeping children at the prison and with research evidence that shows that the first three years, especially the first year, is the critical period in the

------

[6] Shepard, Dean, and Zemans, Eugene S.: *Prison Babies.* Chicago, John Howard, 1950, p. 29.

formation of the child's basic personality and character, serious thought should be given to the task of keeping inmate-mothers and babies together.

Inmate-mothers with babies and pregnant inmates could be housed in quarters separated from the main population. A self-contained cottage would be best but may not be possible.

Each inmate-mother should be primarily responsible for her own child. However, during the day, a nursery should be available so that inmates could pursue regular courses of study and work. Courses in child care, nutrition, homemaking, etc. should be required curriculum for all residents of this specialized cottage.

In the evenings and on weekends, extra help (either inmates or employed) could be on duty to allow mothers a period of free time after the children are asleep.

Crisis Time—Arrest

There should be a routine intake contact with women at the time of their arrest and continued for those in the local city and county jails and for those awaiting transportation to the state prison.

The social services needed at this crisis time could be provided by specially assigned workers from the local welfare or probation department, by the parole board, or by a worker from a voluntary prisoner's aid agency. This should be followed by periodic contacts with the family units during the mother's institutionalization.

Agency Cooperation

The involvement of two or more agencies in relation to a given inmate and her family should dictate that they join in coordinating and planning for the family as a whole, enlisting the participation of all parties to be affected by the plan and its consequences.

Any and all of the above must be predicated upon well-defined policies which are clearly communicated to agency personnel within the given agency. Implementation of policy requires the development of specific procedures and sanctions for their use. Policies and procedures on an interagency basis also are needed, and they should be developed jointly among agencies in order to provide clarity regarding their commitments and expectations of one another as well as to permit their formulation within the reality of limits and possibilities of agency function, legal requirements, and personnel skills.

There is a great need to establish an interagency liaison by persons charged with specific responsibility for doing so. The objectives of such a liaison would be to insure interagency communication and exchange of important case information pertaining to the client-families being served; family-oriented planning of agency activity on a case-by-case basis, with joint participation by all agencies involved, leading to the promotion and coordination of the planning and services provided by the separate agencies; interpretation of policy, procedures, and work problems of other agencies; and continuity and review of planning despite worker and caseload turnover. Agency personnel in the institution and in the field should receive training, orientation, supervision, and ongoing consultation in family-oriented and interagency concepts and techniques that have special bearing on family situations where the mother of a minor child is imprisoned.

Consideration should be given to the establishment of an interagency working committee, representing all the agencies concerned with the various individuals and units of the inmate's family. Such a committee would be charged with developing interagency policy and procedures, for offering solutions to the problems that occur in implementing them, for periodically reviewing and reevaluating internal and external factors affecting implementation of the policy and procedures, and for modifying or establishing new policy as needed. It may be that committees should be established on more than one working level— e.g. a statewide committee and local working committees.

Conclusion

A significant number of minor children are affected by the imprisonment of the mother. Agencies frequently spend public funds to meet the financial needs of such persons, with little coordination of efforts by such governmental agencies. Such a lack of coordination and joint planning can defeat treatment efforts and consequently, harm the children as well as the confined mothers.

SUMMARY

A problem unique to women's prisons is the unresolved question of what to do with pregnant inmates, the babies born while the mother is incarcerated, and minor children of inmate-mothers.

A significant number of minor children are affected by the imprisonment of the mother. In any women's prison, more than half of the inmates will be mothers of minor children.

The family, especially the mother-child relationships, is viewed by the psychoanalyst as the matrix within which the child's basic personality and character are developed.

Research indicates a strong link between early emotional deprivation (parental conflict, cruelty, erratic punishment, and particularly parental neglect) and the emergence of a psychopathic syndrome.

The inmate-mother's own rehabilitation and adjustment are sharply affected by her maternal role and her continuing relationship relative to her children. Unless there is clarification and stabilization of the role she is to play in the rearing of her children, she will be faced with demands and crisis that adversely affect her ability to utilize the institutional program or successfully complete parole.

While many inmate-mothers have personal histories which raise serious doubts as to their abilities to provide adequate mothering for their children, they usually express interest and concern about their children, and these expressions are strongly supported by institutional culture. Thus the mothers might be amenable while incarcerated to offers of child welfare services that would help resolve the future mother-child relationship. Inmate-mothers and their children have the same needs for child welfare services as other mothers and children, but child welfare agencies tend to think primarily in terms of terminating the formal relationships of inmate-mother and child—usually without adequate knowledge of the mother's circumstances, institutional program of treatment, and probable length of confinement.

Females seem to be incarcerated for shorter periods of time than males. The average length of stay at the California Institution for Women was twenty-two months,[7] but inmate-mothers tended to be sentenced to slightly shorter terms than did nonmothers.

Even though many inmate-mothers have been less than responsible or adequate while living in the community, they are nevertheless in a position to sabotage otherwise sound and realistic plans for child care.

The primary objective of this proposal is to help each prison formulate certain policies, procedures, and services to meet the needs of women inmates and their families. Certain basic questions must be taken into account, such as the following:

1. What happens to babies born to pregnant inmates?
2. What happens to minor children of a mother convicted of a felony and sent to prison?
3. What agencies provide social welfare services to inmate's families?
4. To what extent are the services coordinated?

Most families of inmates require certain services, casework, or other helping methods to resolve or alleviate social needs. The most critical requirements are in the following four main areas:

1. Assistance in the placement of children.
2. Assistance in the development of realistic short- and long-term family goals and plans.
3. Assistance to the mother in working out her feelings toward her children, especially where relinquishment for adoption or other arrangements for long-term custody by others is involved.
4. Referral of any of the family members to social welfare resources providing such specifically needed services as medical care, child guidance, group work, and recreation services.

Personnel in all of the pertinent agencies need to become more aware of the following things:

1. The impact on the children and on the imprisoned mother of the

---

[7] *Ibid.,* Zalba, p. 37.

nature, meaning, and consequences of this kind of separation.
2. The importance of some degree of normalization of expectations of the inmate, her family, and other relevant persons concerning visits, letters, gifts, financial support, etc., both during the mother's incarceration and following her release.
3. The existence and utilization of community and other resources that can and should be mobilized in order to achieve solutions that are as effective and wholesome as possible.

An interdepartmental guide setting forth state policy and procedure for the care of minor children of women prisoners needs to be developed in most states.

Assuming that the prison, because of its concern with the inmate and her total family situation, takes the lead in developing cohesive family-oriented planning, the following areas of concern are brought to the reader's attention:

1. There should be the provision of guardianship services to insure that the children of incarcerated mothers are adequately protected.
2. With a law that makes provision for keeping children at the prison and with research evidence that shows that the first three years, especially the first year, is the critical period in the formation of the child's basic personality and character, serious thought should be given to the task of keeping inmate-mothers and babies together.
3. There should be a routine intake contact with women at the crisis time of their arrest, and continued for those in the local city and county jails and for those awaiting transportation to the state prison.
4. The involvement of two or more agencies in relation to a given inmate and her family should dictate that the agencies join in coordinating and planning for the family as a whole, enlisting the participation of all parties to be affected by the plan and its consequences.
5. Consideration should be given to the establishment of an interagency working committee, representing all the agencies concerned with the various individuals and units of the inmate's family.

A significant number of minor children are affected by the imprisonment of the mother. Agencies frequently spend public funds to meet the financial needs of such persons, with little coordination of efforts by such governmental agencies.

It seems imperative, then, for the sake of the children and the mother, that joint planning be initiated and carried through with agency as well as client participation.

BIBLIOGRAPHY

Books

Governor's Council Committee on Rehabilitation: *Guide for Cooperative Staff Work With Prisoners or Parolees and Their Families Receiving Aid to Needy Children.* Prepared by the Classification and Treatment Division of the Department of Corrections, and the Aid to Needy Children Bureau of the State Department of Social Welfare, Sacramento, 1959.

McCord, William, and McCord, Joan: *The Psychopath.* Princeton, Van Nostrand, 1964.

Schapps, Myra R.: *High Walls and Open Gates.* California, 1959. (Mimeographed.)

Shepard, Dean, and Zemans, Eugene S.: *Prison Babies.* Chicago, John Howard, 1950.

State of California Department of Social Welfare: *Parental Behavior In ANC Families.* Prepared by ANC Task Group on Behavior, Sacramento, 1960.

Zalba, Serapia R.: *Women Inmates and Their Families.* Los Angeles, Delmar, 1964.

Articles and Periodicals

Cassell, Russell N., and Van Vorst, Robert B.: Psychological needs of women in a correctional institution. *American Journal of Correction,* January-February, 1961, pp. 22-24.

Chapter 8

LESBIANS

T HIS SUBJECT HOLDS A morbid fascination for the general public and, unfortunately, for many prison personnel as well.

Very little has been written and very few definitive studies have been made on women's prisons. It is indicative of this morbid interest that of the almost nonexistence of material pertaining to women's prisons, two studies have been made resulting in two books[1, 2] being written, pertaining to the subject of homosexuality in women's prisons.

To find that women's prisons are not seething volcanos of sexual passions seems to be disappointing to a great many people. As a matter of fact, most females survive the deprivation of the sexual outlet and usually even survive transitory lesbian commitments to return to relatively conventional heterosexual lives on the outside.

This is not to state that the problem of sexual adjustment that occurs in all institutions where one sex is deprived of social or sexual access to the other does not exist in women's prisons. The prison administrator is faced with a fundamental dilemma: She is aware of the sexual needs of the population that she is charged with holding and retraining—a population that is physically and, for the most part, psychologically, intact and is, at the same time, sexually experienced; and she is also aware that she is not going to get much support or even a sympathetic hearing from the larger society if she focuses upon the problem of the sexual adjustment of her population.

---

[1] Ward, David, and Kassebaum, Gene: *Women's Prison: Sex and Social Structure.* Chicago, Aldine, 1965.

[2] Giallombardo, Rose: *Society of Women: A Study of a Women's Prison.* New York, John Wiley, 1966.

SEXUAL ORIENTATION

The striking differences between the sexual orientations of men and women in the larger society and the treatment afforded male and female offenders by the courts offers the best starting point for a discussion of sex in prison.

By and large, there is in society a bias against committing females to prison, especially when any alternative is available. Thus a women's prison often has within it women who have either committed major crimes (most commonly homicide) or had long careers in crime and who have been strongly recidivistic. Thus, in a certain sense the female institution is composed of some women who have had no prior link to delinquent life styles and a larger number who have had long-term ties with such a life.

The sexual adjustment of women to imprisonment is strongly linked to the general goals to which most women are socialized in the larger society. Probably the most significant difference between men and women in this regard is that women are socialized in the language of love before they learn about sex, while men are socialized in the language of sex before they learn about love. The consequence of this is that women commonly show considerably fewer problems managing sexual deprivation than do men, and while there is little evidence, one might expect that the frequencies of any sexually ameliorative behavior, such as masturbation and homosexuality, are considerably less frequent for women than for men in prison. There is considerable evidence that such behaviors are less frequent among women in the free society than among men, and one should not be surprised that such continuity would be found inside the prison. In addition, women seem to tolerate the absence of overt sexual activity far better than do men, and thus the rates of overt sexual behavior in female institutions should be considerably lower than those found in male institutions.

ORIGINS OF LESBIANS

Views as to the origin of homosexuality have devoted special attention to the role of the same and opposite-sexed parents.

The nuclear family unit has been taken as the model for appraising parent and child roles and interactions.

Working within this framework, many investigators since Freud have reported that male homosexuals go through a phase of overattachment to the mother figure, which leads through certain pathways to the rejection of females as sexual objects. The contribution of the father to this outcome has received increasing attention in recent years. The combination of an overintimate, close-binding mother and a distant, hostile father appears to be particularly significant in producing homosexuality in males.

In females, an approximate converse has been reported, with the father described as the overintimate, close-binding parent. These parental combinations produce a psychodynamic structure characterized by attachment to the same sex and fear of, and hostility toward, the opposite sex. This psychodynamic structure may be manifested in daily activity, in unconscious attitudes, and in dreams or fantasies.

In a study[3] of twenty-five lesbian girls between the ages of twelve and seventeen, the reversed oedipal formulation that appears to describe many lesbians raised in intact nuclear families was not found.

The most striking aspect of this study of lesbian girls was their family background. Not one of the girls had grown up in a nuclear-type family unit that maintained its stability over any substantial period of the girl's development.

It is sometimes convenient to use terms like "the family constellation" in describing familial arrangements. For this group of girls, a more appropriate term would be the "constellation of rearing." The basic essentials of rearing, e.g. food, shelter, and protection from the elements, were provided by the mother or surrogate, grandmother, aunt or other female relative, or foster mother, but the quality of this care varied widely.

Whereas some female caretaking figure was present in each

---

[3] Kremer, Malvina W., and Rifkin, Alfred H.: The early development of homosexuality: a study of adolescent lesbians. *American Journal of Psychiatry*, July, 1967, pp. 91-96.

girl's life, male figures were conspicuously uncertain, unreliable, brutal, exploitative, or altogether absent.

The data reported in this study indicate that in the case of females, the close-binding father is not a necessary component in the constellation leading to homosexuality. None of the twenty-five fathers could be described as "close-binding." There was no discernible phase of close attachment to the father and no evidence of attachment to a surrogate or substitute father. Dreams did not show hostility toward the mother, as expected on the basis of the above-described constellation. There was conscious conflict with both parents that was sharper with the father if he was present. This study made clear that lesbianism may emerge in the absence of the "typical" nuclear family constellation.

Several lines of evidence suggest that normal sexual functioning requires that each partner respect and value all components of her own sexuality and of the sexuality of the opposite sex. The role of each sex must be seen as satisfying and rewarding and not fraught with difficulties or dangers. For the girls reported in this paper, the role of the female was neither rewarding, satisfying, nor desirable, while the male was dangerous and untrustworthy. Females provided these girls with whatever modicum of security they had experienced in the past. Under the pressure of pubescent drives, they followed the path of lesser (not least) resistance and sought female partners.

SOCIAL MEANING IN PRISON

Homosexuality in prison is quite a different phenomen than homosexual experiences in the outside community. Also, from studies[4] made, the typical response of women to the depersonalizing and alienating environment of the penal institution differs substantially from that of males.

Nearly universally in juvenile institutions and in some observed cases in institutions for adult females, female prisoners

---

[4] Gagnon, John H., and Simon, William: The social meaning of prison homosexuality. *Federal Probation,* March, 1968, pp. 23-29.

appear to form into pseudofamilies with articulated roles of husband and wife, and then, especially in juvenile institutions, extend the family to include father, mother, and children, and aunts, uncles, and cousins.

These family systems seem to arise from three sources. One source is a process of compensation; the majority of females in these institutions are from severely disordered homes, and the creation of the pseudofamily often compensates for this lack. A second source results from the socialization of women who, unlike males who form gangs in self-defense, tend to form families, the basic institution in the society in which they have stable and legitimate roles. Finally, there is the fact that the pseudofamily operates to stabilize relationships in the institution and to establish orders of dominance and submission, the primary model for which women have in family relationships with fathers, husbands, and children.

Since all social systems require some form of articulation which is hierarchical in nature, it is not odd that women model their experience on the institution that they know best in the outside community. There is some evidence that the pseudo-family is not as prevalent in institutions with older females, and it is possible to speculate that in these institutions dyadic friendship patterns are more frequent and may be more similar to those in male institutions.

Inside the context of these familial structures, there is the potential for, and the acting out of, overt homosexual contacts. There are varying estimates[5] of the number of women who are involved in homosexual practices, but this variation is probably a function of differing definitions. Limiting the estimate of overt homosexual contacts to overt physical contact, the rate is about one-half. The estimate yielding a rate of about 85 percent probably was referring to the proportion of the population who are currently involved in roles of pseudofamily structures.

A minor part of the overt female homosexual contacts may arise from deprivation of sexuality, but the primary source is the deprivation of the emotionally satisfying relationships with

---

[5] *Ibid.*

members of the opposite sex and the desire to create the basis for a community of relationships that are stable and predictable.

The overt homosexuality derives somewhat from the convential sexual content role definitions of husband and wife. Also, it derives partially from the fact that a certain proportion of females who come into these institutions may well have experience with prostitution in the free community. This is not to say that female homosexuals become prostitutes but rather that among prostitutes, homosexual relationships are sought because of the degraded conditions of contacts with men.

The processes of induction into homosexual activity in the women's prison is often based on the same principles that one observes in male institutions as part of a search for affection and stability in personal relationships. The homosexual relationship offers protection from the exingencies of the environment and the physical homosexual contacts are less sought for the physical release that they afford than for the validation of emotionally binding and significant relationships.

What may be occurring in the prison situation may not be a problem of sexual release but rather the use of sexual relationships in the service of creating a community of relationships for satisfying needs for which the prison fails to provide in any other form. Female inmates tend to create family structures in an attempt to ward off the alienating and disorganizing experience of imprisonment; the homosexual relationships are merely part of the binding forces of these relationships.

The problem for the prison administrator then becomes considerably more complex than merely the suppression of sexual activity—it becomes a problem of providing those activities for which the homosexual contacts are serving as substitutes. The inmates are acting out their needs for self-expression, control over their own behavior, affection, and stability of human relationships. The homosexual relationship provides one of the few powerful ways of expressing and gratifying these needs.

SUMMARY

The sexual adjustment of women to imprisonment is strongly linked to the general goals to which most women are socialized in the larger society. Women seem to tolerate the absence of overt sexual activity far better than do men, and thus the rates of overt sexual behavior in female institutions should be considerably lower than those found in male institutions.

Views as to the origin of lesbianism have followed two main lives. One viewpoint has emphasized the reversed oedpial formulation, with the father described as the overintimate, close-binding parent, in an intact nuclear family. More appropriate to the prison population would be the viewpoint describing the constellation of rearing, whereas some female caretaking figure was present in each girl's life, but male figures were conspicuously uncertain, unreliable, brutal, exploitative, or altogether absent.

Twenty-five lesbian girls between the ages of twelve and seventeen were investigated, with special emphasis on family background and parent-child relationships. This group of girls differed from the subjects of many other reported studies of homosexuality in that (a) the majority had not sought treatment and (b) all were drawn from schools serving predominately lower socioeconomic class populations.

Previous studies had reported constellations of background factors among male and female homosexuals that were approximate mirror images. For females, this constellation includes a close-binding father and a dominant puritanical mother. In this study, the fathers were not close-binding but hostile, exploitative, detached, and absent. The mothers were not dominant but mainly overburdened and hardly adequate for their responsibilities.

The reversed oedipal formulation that appears to describe many lesbians raised in intact nuclear families was not found among this group of lesbians. The findings suggest that the homosexual pattern should be regarded as a final common pathway that may be reached from several different directions. The mechanisms that produce the end result consist not of a relatively limited number of causes but rather of interlacing causal networks that include many varying factors. This study seems to be the most valid assumption of the causes of lesbianism in any population of female inmates.

Homosexuality in prison is quite a different phenomenon than homosexual experiences in the outside community. In prison, homosexuality is partly a parody of heterosexuality. The relationships are conceived of as pseudomarriages, and the women who take part in the homosexual performances conceive of themselves, and wish others to conceive of them, as purely heterosexual. In these relationships, one element is certainly a search for meaningful emotional relationships that have some durability and which serve as a minimal substitute for affective relationships that they normally have on the outside.

If the sexual problem in the prison is not adequately controlled, inmates may develop relationships which leave them open to exploitation or which create problems of jealousy. When a relationship deteriorates or when a transfer of affection takes place, there is a distinct possibility of violence.

Considering the conceptualization of the pattern of homosexuality in the prison, an acceptable psychosexual adjustment of the staff is imperative. Because staff influence is so profound over inmates, homosexual or lesbian tendencies in any staff member should be grounds for dismissal.

BIBLIOGRAPHY

Books

Giallombardo, Rose: *Society of Women: A Study of a Women's Prison.* New York, John Wiley, 1966.
Ward, David A., and Kassebaum, Gene G.: *Women's Prison.* Chicago, Aldine, 1965.

Articles and Periodicals

Gagnon, John H., and Simon, William: The social meaning of prison homosexuality. *Federal Probation,* March, 1968, pp. 23-29.
Kremer, Malvina W., and Rifkin, Alfred H.: The early development of homosexuality: A study of adolescent lesbians. *American Journal of Psychiatry,* July, 1967, pp. 91-96.

Chapter 9

DISCIPLINE

$\mathbf{T}$HE IMMEDIATE CONCERN in prison discipline is with procuring conformity of inmates to the behavior required of them for smooth functioning of the institution. Discipline is an essential for efficiency in the operation of a prison.

When the program of a woman's prison is constructive, disciplinary problems are greatly reduced. With the small population in women's prisons, friendly relations between staff and inmates will allow the emphasis to fall on self-discipline. Loss of privileges will often be the only disciplinary measure necessary.

When harsher disciplinary measures are necessary, the means of deciding these measures must be considered. Whether penalties should be determined by the offense or by the offender is the question of how, specifically, rules and infractions can be defined and how rigorously they should be followed. This usually is put in terms of the officer's "going by the book," versus depending upon his own judgment in determining what constitutes an infraction and how it should be handled.

FLEXIBLE-RULE DISCIPLINE

One method of discipline is the flexible-rule and constructive-penalty approach. Because objectionable behavior by inmates is so diverse that no set of rules will encompass it all without being so long and complex as to be difficult to apply or so arbitrary as to arouse resentment by dealing similarly with highly diverse acts, strain in inmate-staff relationships is minimized by a policy of flexible rules interpreted to fit each case, taking into account primarily the probable effect of each penalty on the future behavior of the offender.

Also, the administration of disciplinary penalties is most effective if it simultaneously does the following:

1. Minimizes alienation of the rule-violating inmate from staff.
2. Maximizes the inmate's alienation from inmate supporters of the infraction.
3. Promotes in the inmate a clear regret over having committed the infraction.
4. Provides the inmate with a perception of clearly available opportunities to pursue a course of behavior which will restore her to good standing in the prison and give her a more favorable self-conception than she has as a rule violator.

With this flexible approach, a minimum number of broad rules can, *if administered by a well-trained staff*, generally be "sold" to most inmates as necessary to maintain order in the institution. Of course, the enforcement of any rule should not depend on its being approved by the inmates. Nevertheless, it follows from any conception of rehabilitation as a change in a woman's inner values that discipline rehabilitates inmates most in the long run of their lifetime, and probably most improves their behavior in prison as well if the rules become internalized as their personal moral opinions. If rules are accepted only as a part of the restrictions of the immediate environment to which one must learn to adjust in order to avoid penalties, there is no interest in following them when the environment changes or whenever the risk of being caught and punished is considered negligible.

This flexible type of discipline calls for a government of man, not laws, in the prison in order to achieve its primary goal, that of rehabilitating offenders through relationships between staff and inmates. With good staff it is possible to achieve a consensus among most staff and inmates as to what handling of infractions is fair and constructive, even when the handling is quite flexible. Of course, any prison staff has some limits to its behavior set by law, both statutory law and administrative regulation. The issue is how much latitude these laws and regulations should allow staff.

It is obvious that this type of discipline depends upon the existence of a prison staff of high calibre. Flexible handling of disciplinary infractions requires keen judgment by staff and an ability to suppress hostile impulses and prejudices. In a prison with staff such as prevail in some federal and in some of the

better state prison systems, flexible disciplinary policy may enhance prison order and also augment the rehabilitative influence
of inmate-staff relationships.

DISCIPLINE "BY THE BOOK"

Another type of discipline is the very specific regulation of
discipline by rules. This can be summarized by disciplinary
penalties which are by the offense rather than by the offender,
and interpreted "by the book" rather than flexibly, create shared
expectations in staff and inmates as to what penalty is prescribed
by agencies beyond the control of the officers confronted with
the offense so the inmate does not become hostile toward the
staff because of it.

This implies that when the offender commits an infraction,
she knows what penalty to expect if she is caught, and she feels
that the staff is obliged to impose this penalty on her should
they catch her, regardless of how friendly they may feel toward
her. Actually, such shared expectations could also occur with
penalties which varied "by the offender," but under explicit rules,
such as one penalty on the first infraction and increasing penalties
specified for those with given numbers or frequencies of prior
infractions.

With this type of discipline, administrative regulations fixing
penalties for each infraction would minimize strain in such
inmate-staff relationships that contribute toward rehabilitation,
for the officers directly involved in the discipline would not be
considered for the penalties.

Nuisance infractions, involving little serious threat to prison
order, such as those from careless habits in putting away equipment or clothing, or doing work wrongly, could easily be administered under this fixed rule of discipline. The fixed penalties
imposed probably would not be such as to seriously alienate the
offender from staff if imposed uniformly, and the infractions
are such as are not likely to receive appreciable inmate support.

When dealing with major infractions, the flexible type of
discipline might be more advantageous. It has been found that
incapaciting penalties, such as solitary confinement in idleness,

rapidly lose effectiveness as they are prolonged. The first one to three days of such an experience seem to have much more impact than subsequent days.[1]

The first day or few days of solitary confinement seem useful in influencing the inmate's communication to staff—but not to infraction-supporting inmates—during this period, and removing her from all diverting stimuli. This gives the staff time to complete their investigation of the infraction and of the offender's attitude. During this time, the staff, in their talks with the inmate, may be able to evoke in her a willingness to cooperate in a program in which her prison activities may be somewhat restricted. Where such a response is not elicited, she may have to be held for some time in close custody, which in most women's prisons is solitary confinement. In this case, diet and certain other restrictions may be lifted.

Research to compare custodial with treatment-oriented prisons would consist of the gradual alteration of disciplinary policies by the prison. This should be accompanied by the compilation of statistics both on prison behavior and on the postrelease criminality of rule violators, before and after the disciplinary change. This change can be undertaken piecemeal by cautious administrators, with respect to only a few types of infractions at a time.

Prison staff have the power to be tyrannical, and where they lack the qualification and training to use this power wisely, a government by rigid laws may be most appropriate. Indeed, in a prison operating under a primitive tradition, with poorly selected, sadistic, or relatively untrained or improperly trained staff, overall introduction of the flexible discipline policy might be disastrous.

When a custody-oriented prison environment is being changed to a treatment-oriented environment, the shift is not to less control, but rather a change to a different type of control. Treatment-oriented personnel must become custody conscious, and custody-oriented personnel must become enlightened custody.

––––––

[1] Glaser, David: *The Effectiveness of A Prison and Parole System.* New York, Bobbs-Merrill, 1964, p. 180.

DISCIPLINARY CLASSIFICATION

A major theme of modern criminal and correctional law is that confinement should vary according to the attributes of the offender: probation, the indeterminate sentence, judicial discretion in sentencing, and parole serving as alternative, complementary, or supplementary devices for achieving such variation.

Using this trend in the law to stress the offender rather than the offense, a classification of inmates within the closed and limited social world of the prison can be used effectively toward motivating inmates to conformity with institution rules. This can also be a means of restricting the communication potential of presumed antirehabilitative or custodially dangerous inmates. Not only may these inmates be retained in closer custody, but the incentive of movement to a higher grade of trustee leads inmates to avoid "troublemakers."

An "honor" housing unit may often contribute more to the comfort of both the inmates and staff than to the reformation of the inmates. One would expect extreme honor programs to be corrupted most frequently by youthful inmates; with these inmates, group pressures for conformity to the most delinquent behavior suggested are likely to be greatest, and are most readily enforced by violence if there is no surveillance.

One cannot equate staff permissiveness with rehabilitative treatment, for where staff permissiveness includes nonsurveillance, it may simply create a power vacuum which the more prisonized components of the inmate population will fill. Inmate surveillance replaces staff surveillance, and inmate life may become less permissive in terms of the freedom available to choose between alternate modes of behavior.

Certainly, reduction of formal surveillance is appropriate in the development of inmate responsibility, but the complete elimination of inmate-staff contact in quarters arbitrarily impedes informal surveillance by staff and blocks the development of reformative personal relationships between staff and inmates.

In an honors-cottage situation in a women's prison, if a prolonged and complete daily escape from staff observation and from staff communication and manipulation is permitted, the opportunity to manipulate inmates then falls into the hands of those inmates in the cottage most opposed to staff-promoted values. The behavior most visible to inmates as representing the expectations of other inmates will be the behavior of the most delinquent components of the inmate population.

An opposite approach in custody housing involves the distribution of many types of inmates in housing and work units so that there is nowhere a concentration of inmates reinforcing each other in antirehabilitative attitudes who might dominate the situation.

A check of the consequences of custodial grading systems should be a routine part of prison-records analysis. It should compare the records of women during the months preceding their entrance into an honor or trustee status with their records thereafter. For these comparisons, a variety of objective indices of rehabilitative progress might well be tabulated, including educational advancement, work ratings, letter writing, and other variables. Patterns of change in performance with change in status, using several independent performance indexes, would be most convincing. However, evaluating women in different status or housing units will be pointless if they are permitted to commit infractions without staff knowledge.

Although women's prisons must admit all ages of offenders, including the entire range of crimes, there can be advantages in this situation.

Separate institutions for men gradually were established for younger offenders because they were presumed to be more innocent, less responsible for their offenses, or more salvageable than the fully mature criminals. Actually, however, an inmate's age and her prospects of continuing in crime are inversely related. The younger inmates are more likely to revert to crime when released than are the older prisoners.[2]

The tendency of youthful offenders to band together and form their own social world indicates that socialization, rather than isolation, is predominant among younger inmates.

Since the predominant flow of advice among inmates is from older inmates to the younger ones, this tendency might usefully be exploited in the housing of inmates. Such applications need

---

[2] *Ibid.,* p. 157.

not mean that younger offenders should be placed with those older offenders who are more confirmed in criminality. Older first offenders or other older inmates not professionally oriented to crime and not highly institutionalized may be an extremely useful influence in the rehabilitation of younger inmates.

Younger inmates more salvageable probably are those with some period of good work record in the past. Those who show some deference to older persons are likely to be most amenable to help. Psychologically, the older inmates may also influence younger inmates by serving as mother figures.

UNIFORMS TO DESIGNATE TRUSTEES

In a women's prison, varying positions of trust can be designated by the color of the inmate's dress. For example:

1. Honor Grade inmates might wear pink uniforms with an H G patch on the sleeve.
2. Trustees might wear green uniforms.
3. Probationary inmates might wear the uniform already in use by the prison, such as blue or white uniforms.
4. Those inmates in disciplinary status, or high security risks, might wear grey or black striped dresses.

These same colors would be repeated in the blouses used with blue jeans.

Along with the color of the uniform, special privileges are extended to those in Honor Grade and Trustee status, while those in Disciplinary status forfeit certain privileges.

One of the main standards by which to judge an inmate's classification should be her conduct and attitude. An inmate's associates within the prison would also influence her classification. The degree of security deemed necessary for any particular inmate must be considered. Conduct and attitude would determine the loss of or return to Trustee and Honor Grade status.

A Trustee would be an inmate who can be trusted, who has a good attitude towards matrons and guards, who is willing to cooperate in all programs, and who has a helpful attitude toward other inmates.

An Honor Grade inmate would have the attributes of a Trustee plus contributing to the good of the institution by doing more than that expected of a Trustee.

When an inmate loses her status by being put into solitary confinement, she should have to earn her way up from disciplinary stripes.

Criteria for eligibility for progression may be based on an inmate's sentence. For example:

1. If her sentence is for one year, she may be eligible to move from Probationary to Trustee in four months time.
2. If her sentence is for two years, she may be eligible in five months.
3. If her sentence is for three years, she may be eligible in six months.
4. If her sentence is for four years, she may be eligible in seven months.
5. If her sentence is for five years or more she may be eligible in eight months.

An indefinite sentence could be based on the lowest number; for example, a one- to five-year sentence could be eligible by four months.

Honor Grade status should be a special category into which few inmates are classified. Possibly as many as one half of the inmate population may earn the Trustee status. All new inmates enter the prison in the Probationary status, unless they are grave security risks. Security risks should be kept in Disciplinary status for identification purposes.

SOLITARY CONFINEMENT

In women's prisons there are no transfers to closer-custody or maximum-security institutions. Therefore, arrangements must be made to handle disciplinary problems, escape risks, and the more emotionally disturbed inmates within the women's prison.

In the last few years, women's institutions are finding that they are receiving a more disturbed, acting out, aggressive type of woman often of a lower age group. These women, it has been discovered, have to be taught how to live in the traditional open institution. Closer structure has to be arranged for them during this learning process.

Temporary segregation, consisting of being kept in one's room for a short time, can be a cooling-off period for the inmate as well as the staff and if this is used selectively, can be effective in putting the inmate in a position to want assistance with her problems.

At the time of a violent temper tantrum and/or acting out on an unacceptable level, segregation in a secure place stripped of any equipment that could be damaged or with which the inmate could harm herself is most necessary. Every women's institution should have a section of a building, if not a separate building, no matter how infrequently used, available for this type of disturbed inmate.[3]

ESCAPE PLANS

Every prison should have appropriate escape plans. These vary with the place of the escape and the time elapsed before the escape is discovered. All plans have certain elements in common. Each shift would have certain tasks assigned to certain officers, in case of escape. For example:

1. One officer would notify police officials and the F.B.I.
2. Another would see that photographs and fingerprints are available to these agencies.
3. Still another officer would call aside likely informants for interrogation as to the course and probable destination of the escapee.
4. Another would make a thorough search of the escapee's personal belongings for clues as to her possible destination.
5. Others would make appropriate patrols of the institution grounds and surroundings.

An appropriate escape plan, quietly and efficiently put into effect at the time of an escape, can reduce the probability of hysterical tightening of the whole institution and of the establishment of new restrictions on everyone.

SUMMARY

The immediate concern in prison discipline is with procuring conformity of inmates to the behavior required of them for smooth functioning of the institution.

---

[3] The American Correctional Association, *Manual of Correctional Standards*, p. 566.

There are two types of discipline: flexible-rule discipline and regulation of discipline by rules.

With a policy of flexible rules interpreted to fit each case, taking into account primarily the probable effect of each penalty on the future behavior of the offender, strain in inmate-staff relationships should be minimized. However, this type of discipline requires a well-trained staff possessing the ability to suppress hostile impulses and prejudicies.

Disciplinary penalties which are by the offense rather than by the offender and interpreted "by the book" rather than flexibly create shared expectations in staff and inmates as to what penalty is prescribed by agencies beyond the control of the officers confronted with the offense so the inmate does not become hostile toward the staff because of it.

When classifying inmates for housing assignments, care must be taken that staff supervision is adequate in "honor" housing to prevent corruption by the more prisonized components of the inmate population.

Uniforms may be used to designate various positions of trust within the inmate population. Standards to judge eligibility to these positions, as well as privileges that are earned in each status, should be developed.

Every women's prison should have a section of a building, if not a separate building, no matter how infrequently used, available for disturbed inmates. Medical staff should make a daily check on inmates in Locked status.

An appropriate escape plan, quietly and efficiently put into effect at the time of an escape, can reduce the probability of hysterical tightening of the whole institution and of the establishment of new restrictions on everyone.

Order in a prison is a collective event rather than the behavior of any few individuals. It reflects the overall patterns of relationships between staff and inmates, as well as intrastaff and intrainmate relationships. Without good security and discipline, there can be no treatment program.

BIBLIOGRAPHY

Books

Glaser, Daniel: *The Effectiveness Of A Prison And Parole System.* New York, Bobbs, 1964.

American Correctional Association: *Manual Of Correctional Standards.* Prepared by Committee for Revision of 1959 Manual. New York, The American Correctional Association, 1966.

Chapter 10

THE MINISTRY IN A WOMEN'S PRISON

Being a chaplain in a women's prison is a specialized form of ministry. It takes a special kind of person to win the confidence and trust of women who distrust others because in at least one instance they have proven themselves untrustworthy.

CONVENTIONAL RELIGIONS

Modern organized religion at home in suburbia is mostly indifferent to the prison ministry, which would focus on the deprived and rejected minorities out of the inner city ghettos and the rural slums. Criminals are considered the dregs of society and the least likely prospects for respectable churches. These success-minded religions believe that ex-inmates as parishioners are liabilities, risks, burdens, and problems, which would slow the efficiency of the modern church.

Most inmates are not of the middle- or upper-class strata of society and do not feel at home in the more forward approaches of the old-line denominations. In fact, the conventional religions of the culture are identified with the police, the courts, and the prisons, who have been seen as the "persecutors" for many of the inmates. This can naturally occasion a block against the religions claimed by the established interests.

Most inmates are from the lower classes and are more familiar with the emotionally oriented sects with a minimum of intellectual content. The Pentacostals, the Jehovah's Witnesses, and the Salvation Army are some of the groups not so far removed from the slums and the ghettos. They remember their own and minister to them.

RELIGIOUS PARTICIPATION

In formal religion as seen in the outside churches, women and children predominate in the activities. Therefore, it is not surprising to find within the prison community a group of inmates who show unusual religious fervor and capacity within the conventional framework of established religious expression for the culture as a whole. The response of inmates in Bible classes, prayer groups, and worship services is more vigorous and powerful than is usually found in church groups on the outside. The inmates are not reluctant to take part in religious discussions, to lead in prayer, to give testimonies, to sing, and participate heartily. It is unusual to have lulls of silence or a timid holding back in chapel programs in prison.

As is true of their underprivileged status, many of the women in the prison community have had inadequate opportunities for religious experience and do not understand religion or look upon it as a vital need in their lives. As a consequence, they may avoid the formal religious programs in a large degree and show varied hostility toward religion.

Paradoxically, most of the inmates will check on questionnaires for religion that they are "interested." Almost all will register as being "Catholic" or "Protestant." It is rare to find an inmate who will write down that she is against religion or that she is an atheist. Many who check that they are interested in religion do not attend chapel or show overt interest in religious programming.

REACH OF THE MINISTRY

In one way or another, the religious ministry in the prison reaches nearly all of the inmates, although many may not attend formal services. Some will contact the chaplain only for family problems, some come to the chaplain only to get Christmas cards to send home, some have a particular religious magazine they obtain from the chapel literature rack. Some inmates will come to the chapel only to attend a spiritual song festival. Some will engage in counseling sessions with the chaplain but will not attend chapel worships. An inmate may be summoned to the chaplain's office to be tactfully informed of the death of a parent, child, or other loved one.

PART-TIME CHAPLAINS

Since few women's prisons are large enough to have the services of a full-time chaplain, a chaplain on a part-time basis must be recruited. He must have the complete backing of his congregation if he is to be permitted to give the time necessary to the prison population.

If a community cleric from one of the old-line denominations has the clinical training and the empathy so essential in correctional work, the women's prison would be fortunate if it could recruit him, for the services of such a person are greatly in demand. Through empathy he will understand the religious needs of the prison population. He will be able to coordinate the work and services of the less ostentatious and affluent religious groups.

But to provide only a clinically trained seminary graduate from an established denomination to minister to the inmates would be to exclude many inmates from the "religion" to which they can respond. To be sure, the inmates are diverse and do not respond to any one approach, but to some tie, to some connection, from out of their past which may lead them to a Jehovah's Witness class or a Pentecostal group.

As the part-time chaplain rarely has time to attend in-service training, it becomes the responsibility of the person to whom he reports in the administration structure, the warden, to orient him to the correctional world and to orient the correctional world to him, particularly the prison staff. Because the chaplain must be permitted to move freely within the institution, he must also be aware of the pitfalls which might negate his most sincere efforts.

Adequate orientation should minimize conflict, yet new problems continually arise in an ongoing operation. Workload stress may limit conference time so essential both to the chaplain and his supervisor to resolve situations arising from apparent divergence in philosophy. Yet only by such problem solving can mutual confidence and acceptance be established.

Both the administrator and chaplain must remain flexible and aware of changing needs in a changing population. Each must be able to communicate freely with the other and with other staff members to be adequately aware of the needs of the chaplain's parishioners and to permit the chaplain to serve special needs on an emergency basis as they arise.

The chaplain must be permitted by the administration to be seen as a man of God and not a man of the warden. However, the chaplain must understand the needs for certain restrictions in the lives of his clients.

The chaplain must share promptly with the administration any information significant to the safety or security of those working and living in the institution.

The inmate will recognize the chaplain as a part of her world if he is seen occasionally in the work areas, the school, or the yards. He can help her bridge the gap between her institution life and community life through family interviews, family counseling, and prerelease denominational contacts.

Often the chaplain's greatest contribution to the women of an institution is in what he is and where he is, not in what he says. He is a person to respect, a person upon whom to rely, and a person available when needed.

SUMMARY

Being a chaplain in a women's prison is a specialized form of ministry.

Success-minded religion is identified with the affluent society and it seeks to perpetuate its interests by cultivating the centers of social prestige in order to share in the established advantages. Ex-inmates as parishioners are believed to be liabilities, risks, burdens, and problems, which would slow the efficiency of the modern church.

So the established church leaves the inner-city ghetto dwellers to be ministered to by less ostentatious and affluent religious groups. The Pentecostals, the Jehovah's Witness, and the Salvation Army are some of the groups not so far removed from the slums and the ghettos. They remember inmates and minister to them.

Most women's prisons will have the services of only a part-time chaplain. He must therefore have the complete backing of his congregation if he is to be permitted to give the time necessary to the prison population.

The warden must orient the chaplain to the correctional world, and the correctional world to him, particularly the prison staff. Although he should be permitted to move freely within the institution, the chaplain must be made aware of the pitfalls which might negate his most sincere efforts.

BIBLIOGRAPHY

Carter, Leverne: The chaplain in a women's institution: expectations of a superintendent. *Proceedings of the Ninety-third Annual Congress of Correction of the American Correctional Association.* Portland, Oregon, 1963.

Eshelman, Byron E.: The prison ministry. *Federal Probation,* September, 1968, pp. 37-41.

Chapter 11

PUBLIC RELATIONS

Aᴅᴜʟᴛ ᴄᴏʀʀᴇᴄᴛɪᴏɴs ɪs somewhat of a stepchild to the general public. The average citizen is deeply concerned with the mentally ill and the retarded, and he becomes emotionally involved with the deaf, the blind, and even the delinquent. But the problems with regard to the adult offender leave him cold. He seems to feel that the offender got himself into trouble, now forget him.

What is done in corrections rarely concerns the public, as long as corrections is quiet about it. Given a prison riot, or what is considered a gross error in judgment in the administration of probation and parole, and everybody becomes emotionally involved. Criticism is made, advice offered, and investigations threatened or instituted—most actively by those who have no basic knowledge of the field.

With regard to adult corrections, there is great lack of understanding, much difference of opinion, and a great deal of apathy. However, due to the unusual nature and purpose of prisons and correctional institutions, the general public will be curious and will tend to form judgments and opinions about them. Because of this, correctional personnel can expect to have public relations affecting them constantly. Whether the public attitude is informed or uninformed, favorable or unfavorable, therefore, becomes a matter of concern to institutional officials.

The success of modern correctional programs is dependent upon a favorable public attitude toward inmates and correctional institutions. Citizens possessing a real understanding of the correctional goals of the institution are necessary to help achieve these goals.

It is not the function of a correctional institution to prevent crime; it is its function to prevent the repetition of crime on the part of offenders now incarcerated.

The objective of building good public relations is to promote modern rehabilitation programs and thus help the inmate to a more productive and meaningful life.

POOR PUBLIC RELATIONS

Prisons and the inmate population provide a ready-made source of material for poor public relations. Escapes, riots, and inmate violations are constantly a threat within the prison. Sensational and vicious crimes for which some inmates are incarcerated contribute to poor public relations. Other contributing forces are the closed and restricted nature of a prison, for the public is always wary of the unknown. The presence of towers, fences, guns, and clanging cell doors are in themselves frightening to many persons. When a disgruntled inmate complains to her visitor about mistreatment and deplorable conditions, the public sympathizes and sides with the inmate and tends to believe her rather than the administration.

The complaining inmate will make little progress as long as she has outside support for her groundless complaints. The institutional officials cannot concentrate on the work of the institution in the face of such unjustified outside pressures. As a result, the treatment of the other inmates suffers. Therefore, the institution needs to build enough good will to prevent the bad publicity from sounding worse than it actually is. Confidence must be built in the administration so that their statements are believable to the public.

When a body of good will and good public relations has been built, this will offset or negate the effects of the bad. Then the public will not be so concerned about each item of unfavorable publicity such as an escape or riot, because they will be familiar with the general conditions within the institution, the treatment of inmates, etc.

Institution programs are far from what they should be. The chief obstacle to progress is public misunderstanding, which results in a lack of proper staff, lack of funds with which to hire such staff and secure the necessary equipment, and frequently, administrative indifference.

Even with a well-planned program of public relations, the institution's standing in the eyes of the public is subject to go up and down very easily—sometimes for reasons beyond the control of correctional officials. Nevertheless, the correctional program must continue in spite of these setbacks.

A good institutional treatment program is essential to a good public relations program. Public relations is a supplement to—not a substitute for—a good treatment program. Many times good public relations is achieved as a by-product from something that began as a rehabilitation program or community service program. Often this by-product was totally unplanned and unexpected. Opportunities to build good public relations from such projects need only to be exploited by correctional administrators.

Public relations programs involving inmates should be designed so as to have a constructive effect on the inmate participants and inmate population as a whole. For example, a play should not be staged for the public only, but should be put on primarily for the inmate population with the public invited to attend.

Public relations programs not involving inmates should also add in some way to the overall goals of the institution. For example, efforts to influence legislators should not be directed toward making the prisons and prison administrator more popular but rather should be directed toward informing these legislators of the goals of the institution and soliciting their assistance in providing the means to help further achieve these goals. The goals of the institution should be kept foremost in mind.

DIRECT PUBLIC RELATIONS[1]

The most effective public relations programs will be those in which inmates are involved and in which there is some

---

[1] Bachman, Dave: Public relations in the correctional setting. (Mimeographed). Florida State University, April 1, 1964, SW556—Correctional Administration.

communication or interaction between the inmate and the public. By this is meant that the public is allowed to converse with the inmate, or the public sees and hears the inmate talk or perform, or the public competes against the inmate. This interaction in itself dispels the erroneous image the public may have previously had about inmates and their treatment and brings about greater understanding of the inmate, her problems, and her rehabilitation.

Occasions and gatherings which include inmates and the public groups on an equal basis are the following:

1. *Meetings inside the institution.* Alcoholics Anonymous or other groups are allowed into the institution for a joint meeting or banquet with their inmate counterparts.
2. *Meetings away from the institution.* This would be the same as above except that the inmate counterpart would leave the institution under supervision and attend an outside meeting, banquet, convention, or local community church service on an equal basis with other participants.
3. *Athletic contests.* Athletic contests between public and inmate teams in which the public and the inmates compete on an equal basis.

There are some occasions and gatherings at which both inmates and the public are present but on less than an equal basis. The groups communicate with each other, but this communication may be predominately one-sided. Examples of this are the following:

1. *Inmate performances.* Inmate musical groups can perform, plays and programs may be shown, and other forms of inmate talent and ability may be exhibited.
2. *Inmate speakers.* Inmates or groups of inmates may be called on to speak to public groups on occasion. Inmates may explain certain phases of the institution to touring groups. Individual inmate speakers or inmate panels may be called upon to discuss pertinent subjects before public groups. Inmates may be stationed at public display booths depicting the correctional program to answer questions and explain various aspects of the display to interested citizens.

While this direct communication between the public and the inmate is considered the most effective type of public relations, it will usually reach the smallest number of people.

On the other hand, the least effective means of building good public relations would be situations in which there is no inter-action between the public and the inmates or correctional administrators. An example of this would be a citizen merely reading about a prison in a newspaper. This type of public relations, while being the least effective as far as the individual citizen is concerned, does reach the greatest number of people.

There are certain types of public relations whereby a small number of people are directly concerned, but with maximum benefit achieved. A few hours conducting one person on a tour of the institution may do more to advance the aims of the institution than many hours spent in other ways.

Some members of the general public are by their very nature more influential than others. The professional press is a good example. Time spent with one member of the professional press may well reap immense public relations benefits.

Another example is the members of the state legislature. These legislators and other state officials should be invited to the prison so that they may become personally acquainted with its program and problems. These people should be allowed to talk with inmates, not just selected inmates but those in the general population.

Because there are inmates in every prison who would try to destroy both the program and the personnel, the administration will have to be able to explain this type of individual to the visitor, to offset untruths. However, inmate's explanations of what the program is doing or *not* doing for them is invaluable in obtaining help for conscientious prison personnel.

INDIRECT PUBLIC RELATIONS

Quite essential but less effective is indirect public relations. There may be an indirect interaction between the public and the inmate. In one instance the public enters the institution, and although they have no direct contract with inmates, they are physically present in the institution and will see inmates engaged in their normal routine. Some examples are these:

1. *Group tours.* Civic clubs, school and university classes, church

groups, and others often tour institutions. The manner in which these groups are received will have a great effect on their impressions of the institution. Tours should be well organized and led, complete, friendly, and candid. Organizational meetings and banquets held at the institution are also examples of this type of public relations.

2. *Individual visits.* The attention and treatment afforded individual visitors to the institution, such as job applicants, interested citizens, and members of the inmate's family, will also have a great bearing on these persons' image of the institution.

In another instance, the public will not be physically present in the institution but will see or hear what inmates are doing or have done. For example:

1. *Display.* The public may see hobby and craft displays or other displays of inmate produced and manufactured articles. Correctional displays at county fairs and other events also build good public relations.
2. *Community services.* The public may see the results of inmate labor. The area of community services is particularly important both from the public relations aspect and from the standpoint of the rehabilitation of the offender. Services such as clean-up projects, disaster work, and performing services for nonprofit organizations provide frequent opportunities to build good public relations.

Officials of the institution have many opportunities to provide firsthand factual representations of what is going on in the institution. For example, correctional officials are often called upon to speak at civic clubs, school groups, and conferences. This gives the official opportunities to explain much about the correctional goals and the inmate. Their speaking ability and personality will directly determine the effectiveness of this form of public relations. Films and slides may be used to augment these talks.

These indirect methods of improving the image of the institution are essential, since all of the people cannot be reached by the more time consuming forms of direct public relations. Indirect public relations are less effective than direct public relations; they do, however, reach a greater number of people.

WRITTEN

Written appeals reach by far the greatest number of people. Through written media, many people who would not otherwise be exposed to such information become familiar with correctional programs.

1. *Inmate publications.* These should be just that—written by the inmates for the inmates. They should *not* be a form of propaganda written by the staff, about the staff, aimed at getting staff views to the inmates. These may be circulated to interested citizens. They may also contain articles or poems worthy of publication in other magazines or newspapers.
2. *Special-purpose publications.* Pamphlets, booklets, brochures, written handouts, Christmas cards, and letters may be duplicated and distributed for the purpose of influencing the public.
3. *Business reports.* Many occasions (such as biennial reports) arise for which printed material must be prepared for public distribution for reasons other than public relations. However, with careful planning, these publications can be designed so as to fulfill their intended purpose and at the same time serve a good public relations purpose.
4. *Press releases.* Items of general reader interest should regularly be given to newspapers in the form of press releases. Suggested subjects for these releases are new construction, human interest stories, special events, personal and educational achievements, rehabilitation progress, and so forth. Press releases are difficult to control due to the fact that the professional press may choose whether or not to print a story and also has the option of rewriting a story. They may use only a portion of the release given to them. The press, of course, may find and write its own story about any phase of the correctional program, whether a press release on the subject is given to them or not. Care should be taken to see that responsible officials answer the questions of the press to assure that accurate information is provided.

Correctional administrators do not have to present a false picture to the public that all is well and that there are no problems. On the contrary, they have a responsibility to be truthful, to present a realistic picture of what is going on in the institution, and to admit that there are problems. Such an approach will lessen ill-will and will inform the public that the official is aware of the problems and is striving to find solutions to them.

SUMMARY

The objective of building good public relations is to promote modern rehabilitation programs and thus help the inmate to a more productive and meaningful life.

A good institutional treatment program is essential to a good public-relations program. Public relations is a supplement to— not a substitute for—a good treatment program.

Public relations programs involving inmates should be designed so as to have a constructive effect on the inmate participants and inmate population as a whole. Public relations programs not involving inmates should also add in some way to the overall goals of the institution. The goals of the institution should always be kept foremost in mind.

Correctional administrators have a responsibility to be truthful, to present a realistic picture of what is going on in the institution, and to admit that there are problems.

Direct public relations are those involving some communication or interaction between the inmate and the public. Examples of this type are the following: meetings including the public with inmates, such as Alcoholics Anonymous, athletic contests between the public and inmates, and inmate performances and speakers. This is a most effective type of public relations, but it will usually reach the smallest number of people.

Indirect public relations, on the other hand, are less effective but reach a large number of people. Examples of this type are group tours, individual visits, displays, community services, and speeches by prison officials.

Written appeals reach the largest number of persons. These include inmate publications, special-purpose publications, and press releases.

Two very important areas of public relations should never be neglected. The professional press and the legislators should always be given consideration. They should be kept informed of the status of the institutional program and their assistance solicited in helping to further achieve the goals of the institution.

Chapter 12

TO TALK OF MANY THINGS

Nᴏᴛ ᴀʟʟ ᴇʟᴇᴍᴇɴᴛꜱ in the administration of a women's prison have been discussed in this book. For example, fiscal management as contained in the *A.C.A. Manual of Correctional Standards* is equally applicable to women's prisons.

One suggestion concerning fiscal management: Be able to defend the budget you are requesting. For example: personnel will be one of the largest items on the budget. Be able to explain why certain positions are necessary. In the request for custodial officers, one post being manned twenty-four hours per day, seven days a week, requires 4.2 guards, using a forty hour work week, *not including* sick leave, vacation, or holidays.

DISPARITY BETWEEN MEN'S AND WOMEN'S PRISONS

In some areas and in many states, the disparity between men's and women's prisons is unbelievable. Male directors, male wardens, and male legislators seem incapable of providing acceptable conditions in many women's prisons. Indeed, they often refuse to believe that conditions are anything but acceptable.

It is apparent that many women's prisons can be rescued only through the intervention of women in that state accepting this responsibility.

To name but a few of these glaring discrepancies between male and female prisons:

1. Many states pay female inmates lower wages for exactly the same work as that done by male inmates. This also extends to female employees.
2. Mississippi is the only state that provides for connubial visits, but these visits are allowed male inmates only.
3. In many states, male inmates are allowed to participate in work release, while no such provision is made for female inmates.

4. Male inmates are allowed to go outside the prison to participate in speaking engagements, sports activities, to man exhibits at fairs, etc. Female inmates are not allowed these privileges.

LAY BOARDS

Those women's prisons that are outstanding have achieved this distinction by having outstanding women wardens who have served the institution over a long period of time. Several of these outstanding women's prisons are also under the protection of boards that are separate from the men's prisons.

To be effective, the board for the women's prison must be made up of intelligent and highly respected citizens, free from administrative responsibility. Its contribution lies in its capacity to report to the public objectively on the program and its fulfillment at the institution, to advise the administration, and to express the citizens' point of view to governors, legislators, civil service commissioners, and other related governmental officers who often discount the advice of the officials of the institutions.

This board could be appointed by the governor. The initial board could be appointed with members serving varying lengths of time—for one-, two-, three-, four-, and five-year terms. Thereafter, members could be appointed for two- or three-year terms. Reappointment would be at the discretion of the governor. This type of appointment would secure the continuity so necessary for such a board. Members should be chosen from all sections of the state, with perhaps a total of ten members. Most, if not all, of the board members should be women.

A lay board, to be totally effective, needs to extend its influence and protection throughout all phases of treatment for the female offender—juvenile girl's schools, women's prisons, probation and parole supervision of women, and women in county and city jails.

INMATE WORK AND PAY

All inmates need work in which they may earn some amount of money for personal needs. If this is denied them, they must prostitute themselves to other inmates to obtain certain necessities or extras of life. Some type of work can be found for even the most feeble inmate, in order that she might retain her self respect. *Every* inmate should have some job for which she is paid. Extra money may be earned through the sale of inmate-made craft items.

TRANSPORTATION HOME

Those women released from the women's prison, whether to parole or especially on expiration of sentence, should be transported by the women's prison transportation officer to their point of destination. They should be delivered to the Department of Public Welfare if they have no family to receive them. This is to insure that after her period of incarceration the ex-inmate will be protected during her period of adjustment back into the free society.

USE OF VOLUNTEERS

The use of volunteers to assist in the prison program can be of great help. However, to insure that these people are "conned" as little as possible, a monthly luncheon meeting should be held for all volunteers. These should be mandatory for those working with inmates. At this time, questions concerning inmates can be answered as well as special information concerning other inmates which may need to be known to those working with them.

WOMEN'S CORRECTIONAL ASSOCIATION

Through the Women's Correctional Association help may be obtained in using ideas and projects found to be of value at other women's prisons.

RIGHTS FOR WOMEN IN PRISON

The need for women to protect the rights of women in prison is a grave need in most states. And for many of these states a lay board is the first step toward improving conditions within a women's prison.

Chapter 13

THE CORRECTIONAL TRILOGY:
PROBATION, PRISON, PAROLE

THIS CHAPTER IS written for the information of the administrator or staff member who comes to a women's prison without benefit of a background in corrections.

Types of release after sentencing are frequently confused. Individuals do not differentiate between probation, parole, executive clemency, conditional release, and release at expiration of sentence.

DEFINITION OF TERMS

Probation is a judicial act of the Court. In case of probation, the offender does not go to prison at all but remains at liberty so long as she observes the conditions imposed.

Bench Parole is simply suspension of sentence, without supervision, and really not parole at all but a form of probation.

Parole is the release of a convicted offender under supervision, and under certain conditions, restrictions, and requirements, after she has served a portion of her sentence in prison.

Executive Clemency or Pardon is clemency through commutation of sentence and is granted to correct a miscarriage of justice or in recognition of mitigating circumstances. Pardon is an executive act of grace. Society takes the blame for the offender having gone to prison. Pardon involves forgiveness and is a remission of punishment or treatment. Pardoned prisoners are free. Pardon restores the right to hold office, to vote, to serve on a jury, and to be a witness. It does not restore eligibility to military service. A pardon restores citizenship but does not make an alien criminal eligible for naturalization. In states a pardon is granted by the Governor, in Federal Government it is granted by the President.

Conditional Pardons are granted by governors of some states. They are releases without supervision and cannot be regarded as parole. The condition may be that the offender leave the state, etc.

Statutory or Mandatory Release is release of an inmate after she has completed her maximum sentence, less time off for good behavior.

Maximum Expiration is release without supervision upon completion of sentence with no credits for good conduct time.

PROBATION

Probation is a judicial act imposed by the Court and takes place only as a substitute for incarceration. The offender remains at liberty so long as she observes the conditions imposed. With cause, probation may be revoked and the probationer incarcerated to complete her sentence or a part of her sentence prior to parole.

Probation has been in use for approximately a century, but it has not achieved as wide an acceptance as it should. Many persons are still committed to institutions who could as safely and more advantageously be placed on probation.

The difficulty lies, as a rule, in failure to understand probation. Too many citizens still think in terms of punishment. To them probation is soft penology. The consequence is that many judges —particularly if elected to office—fear to go counter to public opinion and thus fail to use a method of disposition which might have produced far better results and certainly would have been easier on the taxpayer.

Another deterrent to a wide use of probation lies in lack of a sufficient number of competent probation officers. Some courts have an inadequate staff; others have none at all. Many probation officers have had poor training or none. Hesitancy on the part of the courts to use probation under such circumstances is readily understood.

The rationale of probation begins with the assumption that certain offenders are reasonably safe risks in society by the time they appear in court; it would not facilitate their adjustment to remove them to institutions, and the move might well have the opposite effect. Meantime, the community would provide for their dependents. And the effect of such incarceration upon the inmate's family would be incalculable. If, then, the community would not be jeopardized by a defendant's presence and if she gave evidence of ability to change to a law-abiding life, it serves both society and the individual to give her that chance, conditionally, under supervision and guidance.

Certainly the primary duty of the prison is to protect society. However, 90 to 95 percent of all those in the institutions today will sooner or later be released, and then this protection ceases.

There can be no permanent protection, unless the effort to rehabilitate the individual succeeds—unless during her incarceration something has happened to the offender which makes her no longer a threat to life or property.

There are those who say that prisons do not reform, are nothing more than breeding places of crime.

Glaser's[1] data suggests that prison does deter men from crime, and it is therefore punishment. Also, on the basis of very careful analysis, he concludes that their experience in prison *does not* cause "increased criminalization" for all or most inmates.

Most of those who enter the correctional institution for the first time already have criminal records. Where were they bred? In the free world, of course. The institution must therefore try to do the job which society, in many instances, has failed to do: remove the criminal tendencies which society has willy-nilly fostered.

If prison changes a woman from a felon to a nonfelon, then its prime objective has been achieved.

CLASSIFICATION IN AND AMONG PRISONS

The federal system and all better state systems have classification among and within prisons *for men*. Upon sentencing, the central bureau studies the presentence report and all available information, including the F.B.I. report, and classifies for

---

Glaser, Daniel: *The Effectiveness Of A Prison And Parole System.* New York, Bobbs-Merrill, 1964.

various institutions in keeping with age, intelligence, previous commitments, vocational-training possibilities, and family need.

Male institutions are classified for juvenile offenders, young tractable offenders, young aggressive offenders, older tractable offenders, recidividists, and nonconformists.

Within the male institutions, each man is classified for proper housing, medical treatment, vocational training, industrial assignment, maintenance, and educational program.

The institutional programs at the male prisons are as follows:

1. Reformatories offer vocational training, special training, and academic training through the high school level.
2. Correctional institutions offer vocational training that is less specialized, maintenance assignments, compulsory education to the fifth grade, and industrial assignments.
3. Penitentiaries offer some vocational training, maintenance assignments, industrial assignments, and special academic courses.
4. Camps are farm, road, or forestry.

No such classification program as this is available for women in either the federal or state systems. Many states have girls reformatories and women's prisons. However, there are to date only twenty-nine separate women's prisons in the United States.

PAROLE

Parole is the release of a convicted offender under supervision, and under certain conditions, restrictions, and requirements, after she has served a portion of her sentence in prison.

Parole is an administrative act of the executive or an executive agency. The parolee serves the first part of her sentence in prison but is released for the latter portion. She is to remain at liberty so long as she observes the conditions of her parole. The parolee is under supervision until the maximum expiration of sentence and she can be returned to complete the sentence, with no credit for time away, if she violates the terms of her parole.

The parole supervising agency has a right to expect from parole boards:

1. Women who have benefited from training available in the institution.

2. Women who have grown in their abilities to govern their emotions and impulses.
3. Women able to become a part of the community.

The Function of Parole

The function of parole is to restore a measure of freedom to the woman and to give guidance and supervision during her period of transition from controlled to uncontrolled living.

Parole is a major link in the long chain of rehabilitative techniques. Training in prison needs to be followed by a period of guidance and supervision in a normal community. The period *immediately* following release from prison is the most crucial time for future adjustments. The parolee needs assistance in solving many problems on her return to society. Release without proper planning and guidance could nullify any good institutional training that has been accomplished.

Release from prison *should* be at that particular moment when there is the best chance of the parolee returning to the community and fitting into its pattern as a useful citizen—whether it be immediately after quarantine, after a few months, or after many years.

Parole contains none of the elements of Executive Clemency. It has no connection with forgiveness. It is not designed as a reward for good conduct in prison—good-conduct time is given for that. Furthermore, the woman who conforms is not always the one who has reformed. The chief purpose of parole is to bridge the gap between the regimented and closely ordered life within the prison walls and the freedom of normal living.

Theory of Parole

The theory of parole assumes that the judge cannot determine how long an offender should remain for rehabilitation. Release must depend upon a thorough knowledge of the individual and of all factors which contributed to her crime, and an evaluation of her progress while in the institution. Parole is increasingly regarded by judges as adjunct to our judicial machinery. The inmate needs a gradual reintegration within the group for future security.

There comes a time in every inmate's sentence when she is more ready to return to society and make a satisfactory adjustment than at any other single period. A determination of just when the proper time has arrived is based upon community changes, marital changes, employment changes, changes in attitude, and vocational skills. The parole board alone cannot determine when the proper time for release has arrived. Prison officials know best about attitude changes and vocational skills. The parole or probation officer knows best when the social situation is right and can advise of any special community conditions which should be known. The sentencing judge, the probation officer, the municipality, and the institutional staff are all working toward the same goal.

Social Concept of Parole

Is community protection equal to protection by incarceration? If 95 percent of all inmates come out of prison, there are many dangerous criminals who should never be released, but the existing laws make it impossible to hold them. It is a much safer policy to maintain some control through supervision since the inmate will eventually be released completely free. Under supervision the inmate is liable for immediate reincarceration and may be returned before the actual commitment of a crime on grounds not warranting a formal criminal charge. In this way, parole acts as a "buffer" for society.

Parole as a Method of Rehabilitation

Parole is supervision following the artificial life of institutions. By exercising parole, rather than abruptly stopping all controls and supervision, the parolee is reintegrated into free life by a gradual relaxation of discipline. This type of supervision permits a display of initiative and helps to develop a sense of responsibility.

Parole is a more economical method of treating the offender than prison. The best possible supervision is cheaper than maintenance in prison. While on parole, the parolee not only supports herself but also her family, thereby removing them from the welfare roles.

Paroling authorities should have wide discretionary power. Automatic parole is the greatest danger of any parole system. Parole must not be granted indiscriminately without investigation of the case or planned timing of the release. In automatic parole, at expiration of minimum sentence, there is great danger. Some parole boards release too soon too many inmates whose chances of success on parole are not good. Premature and succes-sive paroles may not only fail to deter crime but may act to encourage certain elements to reengage in crime.

Parole was very clearly defined before the American Prison Association in 1916 by Spalding, who said

> The whole question of parole is one of administration. A parole does not release the parolee from custody; it does not discharge or absolve him from the penal consequence of his act; it does not mitigate his punishment; it does not wash away the stain or remit the penalty; it does not reverse the judgment of the court or declare him to have been innocent or affect the record against him. Unlike pardon, it is not an act of grace, or of mercy, or clemency or leniency. The granting of parole is merely permission to a prisoner to serve a portion of his sentence outside the walls of the prison. He continues to be in the custody of the authorities, both legally and actually and is still under restraint. The sentence is in full force and at any time when he does not comply with the conditions upon which released, or does not conduct himself properly, he may be returned, for his own good and in the public interest.

Parole is not an easy way out of prison, but a wise and practical release procedure—the inmate leaving according to a carefully planned program, under supervision, with ready return to the institution when there are indications of probable failure. Obviously it is foolish to expect a person who has for some time been out of touch with the free world to adjust without help and guidance.

Standards for Parole

The following statement, derived from a number of sources, lists various parole standards which serve as a guide to parole work.

1. The purpose of parole is not clemency but the protection of society.
2. Parole should be the method of release for all prisoners.

3. Society should provide agencies to receive and aid the parolee.
4. Preparation for parole should begin as soon as a prisoner enters prison with his whole institutional program, so far as possible, being directed toward his successful adjustment in the particular type of situation to which he will return on release.
5. In all stages of the formulation of the parole plan the prisoner should be informed as to the situation to which he will return, and he must participate in making the plan.
6. Consideration for parole should be automatic and frequent.
7. In choosing the time most suitable for his release, consideration should be given to the following questions which are major: Has the institution accomplished all that it can for him? Is the offender's state of mind and attitude toward his own difficulties and problems such that further residence will be harmful or beneficial? Does a suitable environment await him on the outside? Can the beneficial effect already accomplished be retained if he is held longer to allow a more suitable environment to be developed?
8. Careful preparation of the environment into which the offender is to go is a prerequisite to release and an essential of competent supervision. This requires wholesome living conditions in the offender's own family or elsewhere, a neighborhood in which the prospects of successful readjustment are fair, opportunities for either work or school if needed, provision insofar as practicable against an immediate period of financial difficulty, and an attitude of understanding and helpfulness on the part of those with whom the offender will come into immediate contact. Important, also, is the absence of any unnecessary attitude of suspicion, persecution, or vindictiveness on the part of local police and other law enforcing officials.
9. Parole supervision is casework involving the whole family of the parolee.
10. Parole supervision also involves the active association of the parole agent and parolee in a sympathetic and friendly relationship.
11. The cooperation of needed social agencies should be obtained.
12. To this end, a full knowledge of community assets and dangers is essential.
13. Good parole means trained personnel, free from political influence, of sound judgment but with a sympathetic and scientific attitude, adequately paid, and with caseloads not too heavy. Knowledge of criminology and penology and contagious optimism as to a possible favorable outcome of parole are basic characteristics of a good parole agent.

14. Parole policy should be sufficiently flexible to permit adaptation to the needs of each case.
15. Experiments with gradual release through an intermediate institution involving partial restriction on freedom should be carefully studied.
16. Good parole needs much further research.
17. Most authorities advocate centralized parole administration, but this should not interfere with active participation of the institution in parole plans and decisions.
18. Good parole requires adequate record keeping.
19. Parole cannot be successful unless careful field investigation has afforded adequate facts about each case.
20. Parole prediction, though still in the experimental state, should be carefully studied. Such devices should never be substitutes for individual case study.
21. Parole should not be viewed as a separate process, but part of a continuous corrective program, which in turn is part of each offender's total life experience. To this end, integration of the entire preventive and treatment programs of community and state, as they affect people from early childhood until the end of parole supervision, is required.
22. Parole needs the active support of an informed public opinion. Of special importance is a changed public attitude with reference to the employment of parolees. When a man fails on parole, newspapers, properly informed, may explain the failure in a way to leave the public's faith in the basic soundness of parole intact.
23. Valuable help may be obtained by eliciting the aid of prisoners of selected types in formulating parole.

Standards for Parole Fully to Achieve Its Purpose

1. The paroling authority should be impartial, nonpolitical, professionally competent, and able to give the time necessary for full consideration of each case.
2. The sentencing and parole laws should endow the paroling authority with broad discretion in determining the time and conditions of release.
3. The paroling authority should have complete and reliable information concerning the prisoner, his background and the situation which will confront him on his release.
4. The parole program of treatment and training should be an integral part of a system of criminal justice.
5. The period of imprisonment should be used to prepare the

individual vocationally, physically, mentally, and spiritually for return to society.

6. The community, through its social agencies, public and private, and in cooperation with the parole service, should accept the responsibility for improving home and neighborhood conditions in preparation for the prisoner's release.

7. The parole offender should be carefully supervised and promptly reimprisoned or otherwise disciplined if he does not demonstrate capacity and willingness to fulfill the obligations of a law-abiding citizen.

8. The supervision of the paroled offender should be exercised by qualified persons trained and experienced in the task of guiding social readjustment.

9. The state should provide adequate financial support for a parole system, including sufficient personnel selected and retained in office upon the basis of merit.

10. The public should recognize the necessity of giving the paroled offender a fair opportunity to earn an honest living and also to maintain self-respect to the end that he may be truly rehabilitated and the public adequately protected.

SUMMARY

The correctional trilogy encompasses probation, prison, and parole.

Probation is a judicial act imposed by the Court and takes place only as a substitute for incarceration. Probation assumes that certain offenders are reasonably safe risks in society by the time they appear in court; it would not facilitate their adjustment to remove them to institutions, and the move might well have the opposite effect. Meantime, the community would provide for the offender's dependents. Therefore, if the community would not be jeopardized by a defendant's presence and if she gave evidence of ability to change to a law-abiding life, it would serve both society and the individual to give her that chance, conditionally, under supervision and guidance.

The primary duty of prison is to protect society. However, since between 90 and 95 percent of all those in institutions will be released, this protection stops unless the effort to rehabilitate the individual succeeds. Glaser's data suggests that prison *does* deter men from crime, and that their experience in prison *does not* cause "increased criminalization" for all or most inmates. If prison changes an inmate from a felon to a nonfelon, then its prime objective has been achieved.

Parole is the release of a convicted offender under supervision and under certain conditions, restrictions, and requirements, after she has served a portion of her sentence in prison. The parolee is under supervision until the maximum expiration of sentence and she can be returned to complete the sentence, with no credit for time away, if she violates the terms of her parole. The chief purpose of parole is to bridge the gap between the regimented and closely ordered life within the prison walls and the freedom of normal living.

BIBLIOGRAPHY

Books

Glaser, Danial: *The Effectiveness of a Prison and Parole System*. New York, Bobbs, 1964.

Articles and Periodicals

Rudensky, Morris "Red": After the stretch. *Harper's Magazine*, April, 1964, pp. 180-182.

INDEX